The Combat Medic Creed

My task is to provide to the utmost limits of my capability the best possible care to those in need of my aid and assistance.

To this end I will aid all those who are needful, paying no heed to my own desires and wants; treating friend, foe and stranger alike, placing their needs above my own.

To no man will I cause or permit harm to befall, nor will I refuse aid to any who seek it.

I will willingly share my knowledge and skills with all those who seek it.

I seek neither reward nor honor for my efforts for the satisfaction of accomplishment is sufficient.

These obligations I willingly and freely take upon myself in the tradition of those that have come before me.

These things we do so that others may live.

The Heart and Soul of a Combat Medic
By Dave "Doc" Hilger
Copyright 2023 by Dave Hilger
Wichita, KS

The Heart and Soul
of a
Combat Medic

Written by Dave Hilger

AIR CAPITAL PRESS

www.acpress.us

"In this captivating book, Dave Hilger dramatically relates what was experienced by members of the 196th Light Infantry Brigade during the Vietnam War and the war's effects on fellow veterans. Hilger's extraordinary narrative reads much like Ernie Pyle, a Pulitzer Prize war correspondent, best known for his stories about soldiers during WWII. Hilger, who served both as a medic with Company C, 3rd Battalion, 21st Infantry, and as a medic at a forward aid station, shares his emotionally charged reflections through the eyes of a medic. Altogether, Dave Hilger presents a highly charged emotional and intense narrative of a combat medic."

- Richard Gariepy

Table of Contents

Forward by Dr. Bob Klein

Dave Hilger's book describing his year as a medical corps medic will certainly add to the height of the voluminous literature about the Vietnam conflict, not just the breath of it. His account relates one person's using a discerning eye on the pathos of battles witnessed, trauma to the U.S. military men, South Vietnamese people, and the enemy, Viet Cong and North Vietnamese soldiers. He describes the exemplary courage of all the men on both sides following orders from above. So many dying early in life, why? But men like Fr. Bob Gariepy and other chaplains guided the souls into eternal life. Who knows what their eternal destinations would have been if they had survived and gone home. In Vietnam, they died in the service of others, comrades in arms as well as the oppressed Vietnamese people.

I do not remember exactly when Dave and I met. We were assigned to C Company 8th Support, 196th Light Infantry Brigade and soon worked closely caring for the sick and wounded from 1967 into 1968. I soon learned that somewhere in time and eternity God gave David life….. and saw that it was good, very good. He was smart friendly, courageous, found no task unworthy of performing well, always had a smile. He had outstanding talent when performing lab and X-ray tests and was a man of great FAITH. Together we also filled about 1,374,578 and one-half sandbags that were placed against the walls of our tents for protection.

Cain slaying Abel began the carnage and sadly it continues to this very day. Nevertheless every war contains acts of supreme courage and unselfish acts that tell the story of man's capacity for goodness while in the clutches of horrendous evil. David has been a witness to the evil side and a witness of the conflict. He presents a clear concept of his observations and how his own emotions and memories affected him in 1967-1968 and into the present day.

When my year in Vietnam was up we gathered on the flight line, ready to board. We watched as the Continental airplane that would take me back home landed. We watched as a hundred plus "new" soldiers exited the craft and set foot on the foreign, hostile soil. From my year-long experience in Vietnam I knew a significant number would return home in caskets, others without limbs or with life altering afflictions. So sad!

As our plane lifted off the ground, heading to the U.S, there was complete silence, no cheering, among these war-weary men. I asked my seatmate "why so quiet?" His reply? "I am remembering my friends and comrades and all the men who will not come home." We were all thinking the same thing.

When I arrived in the U.S. I went straight to the restroom and put on civilian clothes. Chicken, maybe. But given the political climate I didn't need any anti-war folks provoking me. I focused on my arrival in Cleveland where I would see my precious, beautiful Karen, son Casey and daughter Beth, born while I was away. You will read that Dave Hilger's return home was a bit different.

Memories of Vietnam as spoken to others must not glamorize the war or make it more violent than it was. The truth of what occurred is very, very important. David's book tells what his memories of his time as a medic was really like. I believe these memories, both good and bad, have made him a better person. The stories we tell about Vietnam come from our memory bank that is still active in us and is all about things that are important to us, even today.

David teaches that there is no doubt that every participant in that conflict harbors memories that affect their life in some way every day. When you meet a man with a Vietnam Veteran cap and talk to him, it is apparent that his days in Vietnam had, and continue to have, great meaning to him and those memories remain alive and well.

Amen.

Dr. Bob Klein

PART ONE: DESTINY LEADS US

My Military Family

My family has a history of serving in the military and the Peace Corps. I like to say we come from a long line of patriots. Three of us boys were in the army. One younger brother joined the navy and another younger brother served with the Peace Corps in South America.

Three family members were officers. My oldest sister, a nurse, was a U.S. Air Force 1st Lt. A brother-in-law, a doctor, was a U.S. Air Force Captain. His son, my nephew, graduated from West Point. As a captain he participated in the Gulf War, going into Kuwait with the armor unit, first wave. Two other brothers-in-law served, one in the army and one in the navy.

Going back another generation, my dad's first cousin, Edward Hilger, was killed in Europe in World War II with the army. Several other cousins fought in the Pacific War and came home to tell about it. President Kennedy's words have always impressed me: "Ask not what your country can do for you – ask what you can do for your country."

Perfect Life

I grew up on a Kansas farm. The daily routine of rising early to do the chores was simply a way of life. I was number seven of a family of eleven. Six boys, five girls. I knew I would not be a farmer. After high school at the local small town, I went right into college. After two and a half years in Army ROTC at college and having been accepted into advanced training to become an army officer, I decided to drop out of college and volunteer for the draft. That decision had been wearing on me heavily since it seemed all the young men I was in school with were dedicated to avoiding the draft.

It was 1966 and the war in Vietnam was escalating rapidly. Knowing many of our best men were there fighting and dying, while I was living the "good life" at college, simply was not acceptable for me. I was impressed how easily and immediately I got orders to report to the Kansas City Induction Center after I told the lady at the draft board in Wichita I was volunteering!

After having made up my mind to "10-49," (sign a volunteer request form), from Fort Riley, Kansas, to Vietnam, I was completely committed and determined not to be swayed by any person or event. From that moment on, I was totally dedicated to the process of "breaking away" from the good life I had grown up with to prepare my every physical and mental fiber for war! The Vietnam War was in a place as far as one could get from home and totally foreign to everything I had known, from their language to a culture that dates back thousands of years. It was a place so far removed from my familiar climate and all the physical luxuries we had come to expect.

One of my biggest motivations was a friend in high school, Larry Lane, who was already over there with the marines in some heavy combat. My basic training was at Fort Leonard Wood, Missouri— "Little Korea." After they shaved our heads, we all looked alike, and that was the beginning of my life as a member of the best army in the world. Our military knows how to make a team member of each man and to instill in him the life-and-death importance of never leaving anyone behind and always covering your buddy's back.

One incident in Basic became a critical part of my destiny, my life in Vietnam. It was in my first week in Basic during a day of training. We were charging on a rocky trail through obstacles when one of my platoon members slipped out on a turn and crashed into the sharp gravel, which tore into his knee. Our platoon leader, SFC Munson, called a halt and had us form up as a group, asking if any of us had first aid training. When I raised my hand, he threw me an aid bag, saying, "Hilger, see what you can do for him." After cleaning up the wound, disinfecting it with iodine, and applying some anti-infection ointment and a gauze pad, and taping it securely, Munson said, "Good job, Hilger, now get back in there." For any of us recruits to get a "good job" from Sgt. Munson was a real ego boost. I was First Platoon's medic the rest of Basic.

After Basic I was sent to Fort Sam in Houston, Texas for Combat Medic Training. I expected to be shipped out to Vietnam soon after, but they sent me to Fort Reilly, Kansas first.

I had a "piece of cake" job at the Army Hospital. I worked in an X-ray clinic from 7 a.m. to 5 p.m. with weekend duty every other weekend. We had a new barracks with real luxuries. There were pool tables and a nice TV room. On Post, we had the usual P.X. (Post Exchange shopping center), several movie theaters, along with a large swimming pool, tennis courts, and a ball diamond. The whole setup was very disturbing and quite uncomfortable for me each time I worked with one of the casualties that had come to us from Vietnam. In every wounded man, I saw that distant look in their eyes—a look that made you wonder about the many unspeakable events that those same eyes had absorbed while in combat in that mysterious land so far from this safe world. The life the army had assigned me at Fort Riley became more and more uncomfortable when I saw what the soldiers in the same army were enduring over in Vietnam.

I had a thirty-day leave coming before I would ship out overseas, and I already had many mixed feelings, initially thinking I would use the time to gradually pull away from my family and friends. I wanted to just get on with it and never look back. My decision had been made after a series of long hours contemplating the pros and cons that tore at my soul. All of this was going on during the seven months I was stationed at Fort Riley in 1967.

The time finally arrived for me to part from my friends at Fort Riley and the comfortable job at the hospital. I would drive my 1962 Chevy Super Sport home one last time to turn the keys over to its new owner. I had pretty much decided to take care of all my loose ends before shipping out. I had just had my twenty-second birthday, and with ten other children, my parents had enough to be concerned about without me adding more.

The days on the farm while I was on leave before reporting to Oakland, California, for my departure to the war were difficult ones. I lived in a constant seesaw of feelings. Some days seemed to last for a week, with my thoughts far away and my heart already free from the torment of parting from my childhood world, having mentally transported myself the 12,000 miles to that foreign world of Vietnam during restless nights.

On one of those still, warm September days when the meadowlark was sharing its song from one of the strong hedge posts that formed the straight boundary lines of Dad's farm, I said goodbye to my little brother Steve. Steve was the youngest of our close family of five girls and six boys. It seemed he was always saying goodbye to one of the older brothers or sisters while staying home to help Dad and Mom with the farm. On that day, I strapped on my favorite pistol, a Colt Woodsman .22-caliber automatic, and Steve grabbed his Daisy BB gun, the one I had carved a new straight-grained mahogany stock for and had cut a personalized S in the base. We headed out through the grove of trees, opening into the west pasture.

We casually moved down the gradual hill behind the barn into the trees

17

and undergrowth. With my brother walking silently at my side, I noticed how he seemed to have grown faster that summer and seemed much more mature. His light blond hair lifted with each slight puff of late summer breeze, and the quiet look on his tanned face made me realize how tough this was for him. Now he looked older than the playful twelve-year-old boy I had known. I knew that in a few days I would be totally consumed by surviving in my new world, while he would be back here looking at all the familiar things of home, things I would never see the same way again…if at all.

He was falling into the accepted way of saying goodbye in our family. It was the way passed down through many generations of our ancestors from the "old country." Family partings were done quietly, personally, and without a big fuss. You simply busied yourself avoiding the subject until the last moment, and then made it short and quick and walked away. We had a warm and satisfying afternoon, finding targets to test our marksmanship. Steve had been a good student; his aim was steady, precise, and on target. I knew he would be okay. As we walked back up the slope to the barn, I saw much of myself and my own childhood in him, his adventurous joy with life, ready to test the unknown. We walked by the barn up to the house as the sweet smell of the summer's hay drifted across the yard mixed with the smell of Mom's wonderous fried chicken, mashed potatoes, gravy, homemade bread, corn on the cob, and a couple of apple pies still steaming on the kitchen countertop.

Mom's meals were always the best, with no shortcuts when taste and quality were at stake. Her life was busy from five in the morning, helping us with farm chores, preparing breakfast, washing, cooking, and baking…lots of baking, until ten or ten thirty at night when she finally had a few minutes for herself. These last minutes of the day were spent on her knees praying, thanking God for the day's work, joys, trials, and blessings.

Dad's days began way before dawn, working a full-time job in town then coming home to manage a farm and all of us. Many of those long, tiring days had to be overwhelming for him, especially when our well-meaning help with the farm work didn't work out too well. Later, as we became older and more experienced, the work was done much more proficiently.

Saying goodbye to one's family when leaving for war on the other side of the world, to a place where there are no more telephones, relaxed evening meals with the family, or even a peaceful night's rest, is tough, right up to the last word. The routine of farm chores and my younger brothers and sister going to and coming from school made most of the time move along. I really didn't have much to say to my friends around home, mainly because they had all gone off in their own directions, as I had. Since I had spent two and a half years away at college and one year in the army, there simply wasn't anyone around to say goodbye to.

The morning Dad, Mom, and Steve took me to the airport was a typical day of morning chores, eating breakfast, and Mom checking off the things I would need, most of which I would have to send back home the first day or two after I arrived! What does a mother and father feel when saying goodbye to a son in a situation like this… I can only imagine when I look at my own son now. Mom was very brave giving me that last hug, with tears on her cheeks, reminding me again to pray every day and asking if I had my rosary. Dad's warm, strong handshake and words of support were touching and strangely final; Dad simply did not shake hands with his sons except at very profound moments.

My brother Paul, who worked for an airline, came over to us then to fly with me to Los Angeles on a first-class flight. As Paul and I turned away to walk out to the waiting airplane, Mom insisted we stop and turn around for one last picture. With the lump building in my throat slowly sinking to a knot in my stomach, I told Paul to keep walking, but after several more pleadings from Mom, we turned for one of the worst photos I have ever seen.

Paul and I arrived in L.A. in late afternoon with one whole night before I was to fly on to San Francisco. After a very "high-dollar" steak dinner

19

with all the trimmings and a long night of hitting some hot spots in the "big city," it was time to say goodbye to brother Paul. How do you say goodbye to someone you have shared everything with while growing up? The good times and the tough times, the hard work...even Dad's car for the Friday night football games! With a firm handshake and a, "Well, I guess I'll see you in about a year," we both turned, walked away, and didn't look back.

This Is Real

It was on to San Francisco followed by a short bus ride to Oakland, where I would spend three days lying on a bunk with a bare mattress in a large barracks, falling out four to five times a day to listen to names called out for flight numbers destined for Vietnam. Finally, on the third day, after sweeping out a large warehouse (army busywork), my name rang out. The callout of my name was followed by a flight number that I saw was scheduled to leave at 5 p.m.

At that point, we were marched to an immediate holding area. It was an open building, big enough to play football in, with cots, bunks, and mattresses scattered everywhere. My first impression of this place was strange, in that it was surprisingly disorganized, unlike every other place I had seen in the army. We were held there for about three more hours, the plane having been delayed several times for one reason or another. The tension built to the point that this large open space became eerily quiet, even with over three hundred soldiers milling about.

When there were only forty minutes to flight departure, an announcement was made for all of us to make one last phone call home. We were instructed to talk for no more than three minutes so that every man could have a chance at one of the thirty phones lined neatly on one wall. I stood in line for a phone, certain that I did not want to say goodbye again. As the line moved quickly, I was torn. I knew I should call home one last time; there was no denying that every soldier there was aware that a number of us leaving on this flight would not return on one a year from then. As the coins falling through the phone gave me a dial tone, I slowly dialed Mom and Dad's number. Mom answered, and after an exchange of greetings, she said that Dad was out on the farm somewhere. She was shocked that I would be shipping out in only minutes. Our conversation was filled with too many pauses, neither of us knowing what to say. Finally, with only part of my three minutes used up, I told Mom that there were a lot of guys trying to make their call and that I had to get off the phone. One more time, I would hear Mom's voice break from emotion. It was not until many years later that I learned that Mom was sure that was the last time she would ever hear my voice.

Words of "Welcome"

October 1967, Bien Hoa

After a long flight over the Pacific with one stop in Hawaii, we landed in the southern tip of Vietnam, Bien Hoa. The outer door slammed open seconds after the commercial DC-8 came to a "nose-squatting" stop, and an army major charged in. He was barking orders as he stormed up the aisle. "Everybody up and out; take everything you carried on board and move out!" We quickly but in an orderly manner pushed toward the door. Almost immediately, the air was filled with tension and the smell of sweaty bodies. The moment my turn came at the doorway, all my senses instantly came alive. The blast of equator heat flashed by my face, carrying a world of smells with it. The air was so hot it seemed heavy; the smell of cordite from the mortar explosions dominated the local native smells— the smell of wood fires mixed with strange cooking odors, the overwhelming odor of people living closely together without a sewage system. We ran in our army Class A khaki uniforms carrying our small, cynically named AWOL bags. Mortars were still hitting but not in our immediate area. There was something about the finality of the krump...krump...krump... sounding like a giant kettle drum, accenting the final act in our young lives. Those mortar sounds created an indelible impression of Vietnam in our minds. We ran several hundred feet with adrenaline surging through our bodies, making every physical sensation imprint in vivid color on our memories and becoming a part of us forever.

The first American soldiers we saw were seasoned, aged combat veterans, sitting along a sandbag wall, waiting for their ride home! They sat with their combat gear on or stacked around them: rifles, grenades, machine guns, M-79s (grenade launchers), and rucksacks. They didn't look like us at all—they were dirty, tired, weathered, and much too old. This was the first time I saw the much vaunted, battlefield-induced "1000-yard stare," and it shocked me. I knew immediately that we had signed up for something that required every bit of inner strength and toughness we could wring out of our souls!

23

The first words of welcome I heard from one of these combat veterans was, "In six months, half of you poor bastards will be dead!" That was shocking enough, but then I made eye contact with one of them. What I saw scared the hell out of me! He was sitting on the ground with his M-16 lying across his thighs, his hands hanging limply over his knees. He stared through me with eyes that were cold yet very sad. He was slowly shaking his head, pitying me for what I had yet to see... His look provoked one of the most devastating feelings I have ever experienced.

Heading to the next leg of our trip, we ran the gauntlet, taking some jeering, verbal flak, but mostly we were stunned by these men, the same age as us but oh so much older! We knew right then that these men were a reflection of our future, a premonition of ourselves when our tour was finished...if we made it out of here alive. Looking back now, I felt then that I was looking down that one-year road, knowing too well that there were friends yet to know and some to watch die, that somehow we survivors would be looking through totally different eyes. Would anyone back home ever recognize me again? Would anyone back home even care? What I saw in those men is what we would see in our own faces after we had finally reached the end of that long, "time-warped" tunnel. They had, as we were about to, skipped those "carefree youth" years and gone suddenly into middle age. Every step we took after that encounter was directing us down that road of accelerated aging. We took each step along the way as if we'd seen or had been there before, when in truth we suppressed the shock within ourselves. There simply were no other options; however, for every one of those disturbing experiences, there had to be an eventual evaluation and reaction sometime later in our lives. For most of us, these experiences became buried under layers and layers of relentless days of trauma and "heartache," to be digested and relived, slowly...and completely...with many tears of the heart.

We were herded into buses like those used for schoolchildren, except these had heavy wire screens on the windows. We asked, just as every load of men asked, what they might be for. We were told in short order that some of the earlier groups got blown up pretty bad from grenades that had been tossed inside through the open windows. We immediately went through an electrifying change from a training environment to a very real hostile world where people all around us wanted to kill us.

Chu Lai – Home Until September 1968

After having spent my first week in Vietnam at Bien Hoa, just outside of Saigon, corralled with thousands of other "new" troops at a place referred to as the 90th Replacement Center, I was ready to move anywhere!

My "anywhere" ended up being on the northern end of South Vietnam, at Chu Lai in I Corps. This was the base camp of the America Division and the 196th Light Infantry Brigade that I would be a part of for a year. The only thing I could find out about my unit was that they were losing a lot of men in heavy contact with the enemy.

The flight to Chu Lai was in a green camouflaged Air Force C-123 twin-engine cargo plane. The flight lasted most of the day and seemed longer since we all sat on our duffle bags on the bare cargo floor with but a long cargo strap in front of each row of men. The strap extended from side to side, a heavy nylon belt that threw tremendous inward pull on the plane's wall each time we took off, landed, or accelerated.

We arrived late in the afternoon at Chu Lai and promptly were led to a small tin holding building on the sandy beach. This twenty-by-thirty foot "hooch" had a raised wooden floor and a corrugated tin roof with rows of sandbags tied across the ridge by short ropes to hold the roof on in the strong wind that came in off the South China Sea. The sides were hinged about halfway up so that they could be hooked up during the heat of the day and dropped when the cool breeze came in off the sea at night. Unfortunately, the builders didn't think it necessary to have hooks to secure the sides down. So as the 90-mph typhoon winds lashed at our new home that first night, the windward side stayed plastered down while the back side simply flapped horizontally—AND NOISILY—with each great blast of wind and rain. I must admit, in looking back now, it was a good initiation to this harsh world. We had no illusions as to what was to come!

Photo 1: Tents on the sandy beach

Photo 2: Sp. Gerald Wernsdorfer

Housekeeping: Materiel and Brothers

After a very long, wet, and tiring night on the beach at Chu Lai, we all fell out at dawn for roll call and for instructions for our first day "up north." After a short "welcome to the 196th Light Infantry" speech, we were told how the night before was kind of unusual, and that the sergeant in charge was sorry we had to sit out a typhoon without any real protection. I was quite surprised. I had just figured that was the way war was: "Welcome to Vietnam. (Welcome to the war!")

We were assigned general-purpose medium tents, green oblong tents that would sleep approximately twenty men, so there were three tents in all. A bunch of new, green troops setting up these large tents was interesting to say the least. The soil near the beach was all sand, so a whole new method had to be used to make the tent stakes hold. We drove them in at a perpendicular angle to the line to create a "drag anchor" and immediately dropped a sandbag over the line in front of the stake. Part of the first day was spent hanging out our clothing, including everything from the duffle bag, since the "horizontal" rain all night had penetrated everything!

The rest of the day, we dug a trench two feet wide and about three feet deep all around each tent. These trenches were to contain the rain runoff from the tents, as well as give us below-ground protection from rockets and mortars. For all practical purposes, it was an ingenious idea to keep the "new guys" busy. The sandy soil simply fell in on the trench constantly.

The next morning, we began our "charger training." This was a ten-day crash course the 196th Light Infantry Brigade gave the replacement troops on booby traps, trip wires, ambush, ambush sites—just guerrilla warfare in general.

There were about sixty of us, a quiet, serious group that made mental note of everything. In this environment, strangers became friends fast.

Three of us were medics in this group, including Jerry Wernsdoffer. We were three scared young medics fresh from the "world." I guess one could say Jerry and I needed each other desperately. When you're quite young, the "unknown" terrifies. We didn't do a lot of talking; we were busy intently learning things that would keep us alive and at the same time avoiding subjects that were heavy on our hearts and too painful to dwell on. Each of us had to live through those long days and tense, sweaty nights, wondering….

Some things experienced in life are burned into your soul and become part of you for all eternity. When you are standing on the razor edge of a twilight world, your senses are so alive that even the smallest word or image becomes indelible. The sight of Joe, a First Platoon squad leader and "point man," walking up to me as I exited the resupply chopper, is as clear today as it was that sultry late afternoon fifty-three years ago. I cannot begin to describe the loneliness, the fear of not measuring up, the "I'm going to die here!" that overwhelmed me at that moment. However, as with all my most desperate moments in life, my Divine Creator sent someone to give me hope. This "Joe," a young grunt two years my junior with a calm, caring look, asked me if I was their new Doc? He was a slim, trim, tough young man of Mexican descent whom I liked immediately, not aware that we would become close friends and brothers forever.

"Yeah, that's right! I'm your Doc."

"Hey, Doc, don't look so worried, we'll look after you. We'll take care of you." These words meant more to me then, and now, than I'll ever be able to tell.

Joe Mendoza from southern California was a soft-spoken unassuming young man with a good, caring heart. I learned to size up a man in this manner from my dad. My father was a man from the Greatest Generation, the Dust Bowl days, and World War II. He lost his dad when he was only three to a hunting accident. He grew up with a stepfather who not only resented him, but made it very clear that he didn't want him around. To

30

me, Dad was a very wise man, especially when it came to reading a man's heart. In those hard times, he was only allowed eight years of formal education, but he earned a master's in survival, the value of honest labor, honor, and love of family. I can still hear him tell us boys, "A man is only as good as his word," and when he shook hands on a deal, it was done!

Joe was a tough, honorable American grunt warrior as brave and faithful a brother as I've ever been honored to know. He represents the kind of soldiers I served with, the very best America had to offer on that "hellish" altar of freedom.

Medic Survival Training

We trained hard and intently those first days. The training sessions were set on the edge of the jungle, with typical pole-supported thatched roofs, open on the sides and furnished with rough benches made from split local trees. These benches told a story of their own, from the smooth, worn edges from previous nervous "new guys." One day, while listening to one of our jungle experts, we noticed an army film crew panning their large tripod camera on us. They followed us throughout our class that afternoon. If nothing else came of this training film, it had to show our youth and tense, serious faces (and later provide a video memorial of those of us who would not survive). Later, the sergeant in charge told us to write home and tell our parents to watch for us on "The Big Picture." (This was a world newsreel-type show on Sunday afternoon back in the "real world.")

None of us was that excited about the whole thing; the boom of the F-4 Phantom jets (a fighter bomber) going out continuously on air strikes kept us quite aware of where we were. The marine F-4 pilots were very much in demand since they flew strike missions for us (the army) as well as for the marine infantry. They would go out around the clock, and we could but wonder how many did not come back. From that first night in Chu Lai, the sights and sounds of war enveloped us all. We had to learn to sleep with the F-4s literally coming in and going out over our heads. One must experience the sight and sounds of this "heavy" fighter bomber landing with an unearthly howl in full flaps, and taking off nose-up as the afterburner exploded on takeoff with a sonic boom, causing the twin side-by-side jet engines to glow fiery red even in bright daylight, to fully appreciate our combat-free living environment at home.

About midway through this ten-day training period, we were issued our combat and survival gear. We went through the typical supply buildings (tin hooches) with long hallways, wth windows on both sides, where a supply person shoved helmet, helmet cover, helmet liner, several sets of jungle fatigues, boots, M-16 rifle, mag pouches, magazines, pistol belt, poncho, poncho liner (camo), canteens, canteen covers, web gear, pack, bayonet, entrenchment tool, socks, green boxer shorts, air mattress, mosquito net—everything the U.S. Army decided a soldier needed to survive here. As a medic, I was allowed to choose between the .45-caliber Colt automatic pistol and the M-16 rifle. I went for the rifle; the range, accuracy, and firepower were far superior. My M-16 had scrapes and shiny spots on its black metal barrel and plastic forearm and stock that made me stop and wonder how its previous owner went home. Having shot Expert through my previous military career, I made sure it was zeroed!

At night, we watched our machine gun tracer rounds, glowing red streaks zipping out of the sky into the earth, and the green tracers of the enemy arching off the jungle floor toward an invisible target hanging in a black sky. Many a soul-searching thought consumed the "new guy" on nights such as these in Chu Lai, 1967. It was the beginning of a year of long days and sweaty, tense nights spent with only sporadic sleep.

It was on one late afternoon the eighth or ninth day at this training site that we all saw our first hard-core grunt (infantry) sergeant. He was your typical "Sgt. Rock." His quarter-ton jeep whipped to a stop in a swirl of dust and fine white sand as he grabbed the windshield to pull himself up to stand on the shotgun seat.

The staff sergeant was in his mid-thirties with the weathered look of a veteran of this harsh, steamy country. His helmet camouflage was ripped, tattered, and faded from many long days in the jungle and hot tropical sun. He was in need of a shave; his jungle fatigues were worn and faded like his helmet, and spotted from dried red clay and sweat. His boots were the most obvious mark of the "grunt"—they were scuffed to the point of being almost white with the raw leather showing, the result of hundreds of hours "humping" through the dense jungle. The heat, and a few beers too many, caused him to sway a little.

Waving his automatic pistol, he began roughly shouting. What he said that hot afternoon burned into my soul and provided my coming-of-age in Vietnam! "How many ******* medics we have here?" Three slow, measured hands went halfway up. "They're killing our ******* medics as fast as we get them out there! You three are going with me.... In case any of you guys are interested, the life expectancy of a medic under fire is six minutes!"

The drive to the helicopter landing pad in this guy's jeep was tomb quiet, with each of us desperately holding back a barrage of razor-sharp emotions. It must be what a condemned man feels as he is led out of his cell for the last time: flashbacks of a life protected under my parents' roof; simple, innocent, warm summer days with my family. The smell of fresh-turned earth and the sweet song of the meadowlark on the farm back in Kansas seemed to consume my mind. From the moment this sergeant barked out his orders to us medics to come with him, Jerry and I never spoke another word to each other. We simply stared into each other's eyes for a long moment, saying all those things that were impossible to say. Our final farewell, and hope of somehow surviving this "ungodly" war, was all communicated through our eyes. This was the last time I would see the sparkle of life in Jerry's eyes. We parted that afternoon without the conventional handshake or words of good luck, sure that we were both dead! He flew directly out to one of our "line" companies, while I was flown to our forward aid station on Hill 35.

Six months later, I would see him again. He came through our aid station on Hill 63, LZ Baldy, on his way home with the rest of the real heroes. He came to us wrapped in a poncho, cold and pale and looking like all the rest. He had been hit twice in the chest by an enemy sniper as he rushed forward in a firefight to aid a wounded squad leader. By this time, I had long since been numbed by the brutal scenes of war. I would put aside the luxury of grieving for a good friend for many years, after the soft, easy life back in "the world" had eaten away a portion of the thick, tough emotional wall that war had strongly built around me.

Jerry had died a hero while trying to get to a fallen brother even though he was aware of the extreme danger of moving in the middle of a firefight.

34

He made his leaden feet and legs carry him to fulfill his personal obligation to relieve the suffering of a fallen brother, knowing all too well his own survival was questionable at best.

Photo 3: Ten day "Charger Training" after arrival at Chu Lai. The soldier (fellow medic) with sunglasses is Jerry Wernsdoffer.

Photo 4: Ship off the coast of Chu Lai. A very interesting view for a Kansas farm boy.

Part Two:
Finding Brotherhood

*I sought my soul, but my soul I could not see. I sought my God, but my God
eluded me. I sought my brother, and I found all three.*
William Blake (1757–1827), paraphrased

Medics Learn Multiple Skill Sets

Hill 35, 1967

The aid tent was a beehive of activity. Medevac choppers were coming too regularly and already we had wounded men pilling up in the dirt-floor tent. The doctors and medics were working like mad, as usual, making me really proud to be accepted as a member of one of these many superb American medical teams in Vietnam. The aid station was filled with scenes of intense pain, fear, and sometimes joy (finding buddies are still alive, along with one's self), tension, and plenty of heartache.

The medical people had many roles to live out. First and most importantly, we knew as doctors and medics, you must see yourself from the perspective of the wounded or dying soldier! It takes training, awareness, and I feel a certain natural (God-given) ability. The hurt, scared soldier will always lock onto your eyes (the window of the soul). No matter what our feelings are, whether of shock, hurt, or deep concern, that injured man can pick up every emotion we telegraph his way. We all became experts at disguising our emotions and true feelings. Those first desperate answers he searches for are usually answered by our reactions or statements. We learned this in our training in the States, but no training can teach like living through it. Sometimes, because of the immediate and urgent need for a new medic, the lack of perfection of this most important skill could cause devastating damage to a badly wounded soldier's will to live. Some of us were able to pick up on this quickly, while others needed training and time working with an "old-timer." An example of this comes to mind for me on one of those days of mass casualties on Hill 35. When the wounded came in chopper-load after chopper-load, it was every medic and doctor jumping in and doing whatever was needed. We tried to visually select the worst or the soldier who was having the most difficulty. I grabbed a large Black grunt with a large field dressing on his left shoulder and upper arm. This day, I had a new medic with me; for whatever reason, he had latched onto me and stayed close to me the entire day. After this incident, I saw that I should have taken a second or two to prepare this new man for what he would see.

The grunt was doing fine standing among the rest of the wounded smoking a cigarette. I cut loose the large combat dressing and gently pulled it away from his shoulder. The whole shoulder was ripped open, exposing the bones and joint. As the wound was exposed, the new medic let out a gasp and a spontaneous remark along the lines of "My God, his whole shoulder is gone." He had unintentionally made this wounded man a potential shock victim. It took considerable reassurance and finesse on my part to get the injured soldier calmed down enough so I could clean the wound and redress it.

Photo 5: Medics in action

Photo 6: More wounded

Clean Kill Mystery

It was a day much like all the others. The medevac choppers came to our muddy little hilltop, Hill 35, from several different directions of the dense jungle. All of them were filled with bleeding, hurting, wet, and scared young soldiers. After a hard race against time and enemy bullets, they would flare in a swirling misty cloud of shredded rain and mud. Their cargo of suffering flesh would come into our aid station tent in varying degrees of severity. Some wounds were seared black from the terrible heat of the flash of modern high-explosive mines and mortars, cauterizing blood vessels. Others were bleeding uncontrollably from jagged chunks of metal, leaving stumps where young, strong arms and legs had been just seconds before. The modern full-jacketed, needle-nose, high-velocity bullets would leave a disastrous path when passing through flesh and bone. These bullets would take an arm or leg off in hitting a joint or would become unstable after striking a bone and shatter or make a ninety-degree turn, ripping a tunnel of destruction through the trunk of the body. These were the wounds we hated the most. The extent of the damage was next to impossible to estimate without sophisticated medical equipment. Some of the most damaging bullet wounds I saw came from our own modern rifle, the M-16. The small .23-caliber bullet travels at nearly four thousand feet per second and would often breakup on contact, or travel in an erratic path through the flesh. Many of our weapons were used against us as a result of our Vietnamese allies' (Army of the Republic of Vietnam, ARVN) units being overrun, as well as our own overrun American units.

It was one of those monsoon days of torrential rain. We had an exceptionally large number of casualties come to our soggy hilltop aid station. There was the usual mad dash to get to the critically wounded first and to sort the lesser wounds in some kind of priority of treatment. In medical terms, it's called triage, a system developed from necessity, urgency, and just plain cold efficiency. The KIAs (killed in action) were unceremoniously stacked off to the side. In this group of casualties, we had three KIAs lying in the mud without even a poncho to keep the rain off them. I remember being quite aware of every detail about these men because they were still warm. This I was acutely aware of the second I grabbed them off the bloody chopper floor. After the usual frantic minutes of dragging litters and bodies off the choppers, I said, *the hell with it* and went to get Dr. Scottie. He listened intently while I poured out my fears and anxieties over the possibility of one or all three being alive…somehow. No official pronunciation of death could be done in combat. It was left to the field medic (a platoon medic, a platoon being approximately thirty men) or whoever was left in command after the smoke cleared. The biggest fear I had as a medic was that we might "bag up" (put into a plastic body bag) one of our men who was in deep shock or a coma and only assumed to be dead!

After a few more minutes of stabilizing the life-threatening wounds, Doc Scottie and I went back out into the suffocating downpour to do a thorough examination of these three soldiers. He checked each man for any sign of life: dilation of the eyes, as he flashed his pen light into them, a pulse, or a faint sign of air movement into the lungs. There were no signs of life; they all proved to be dead. However, I never for a second regretted being insistent about the examination. Dr. Scottie and I had become good friends through many long days and nights in this slaughterhouse environment, and I feel he did it mainly as a favor to me, realizing how important it was for me. As we proceeded with our examination of the three men starting from the nearest, we came to the last man, a young second lieutenant. We became more perplexed as we checked him over. There didn't appear to be a wound or even a mark on him. At that point, we stripped the body, which was washed clean in a few seconds by the heavy monsoon rain pouring over us.

We were finding absolutely nothing to indicate a superficial wound, let alone a mortal one. Dr. Scottie was getting quite intent by now and was checking the man's eyes very closely when he said, "Dave, take a look at this!" He was shielding the lieutenant's face from the rain with his chest as he held the left eyelid up to expose the white uppermost part of the eye. He then produced a long, thin probe (we carried different lengths and thicknesses to locate shrapnel in deep puncture wounds), which he inserted into a tiny, dark spot in the upper portion of the eye. He fed in the probe, with no resistance, for about three inches. The young lieutenant had been killed instantly, perhaps by a small, high-velocity piece of shrapnel that entered his eye and pierced his brain? Or maybe he suffered a fatal concussion from nearby exploding ordinance. Dr. Scottie really couldn't definitively tell what had happened.

Camp Evans, 1968

It was a beautiful, clear morning with a few cotton ball clouds floating in a blue sky, another Sunday at Camp Evans where the NVA hits us with 122 mm rockets several times a day. Since our aid station was near the air strip, it was dangerous to be very far from our bunkers. This particular Sunday morning, Father Robert Gariepy, our "Sky Pilot," was holding Mass for several of us medical people as well as some of our walking-wounded grunts. We had coined him "Sky Pilot" from a song of the '60s by Eric Burdon & The Animals.

The large rectangular wall tent had the sides open, allowing some airflow since it was already hot at mid-morning. Our Sundays were like every other day except those Sundays when we were fortunate enough to have Father Gariepy with us at the aid station. Father was on the move constantly, traveling by chopper, by jeep, on foot—whatever it took to get to our combat troops. He was a major morale and spiritual boost for our grunts, for they knew he cared deeply about them and that he would be there for them no matter what he had to do to get to them. A number of times, he came into hot LZs and even had to crawl under fire after he had landed.

At a recent 196th reunion about 30 years later, I witnessed one of his "grunt boys" locate Father Gariepy and thank him for always being there for them and for the pair of jungle boots he gave him. Father Gariepy was in the bush with one of our line companies when he noticed one trooper from California who had his toes sticking out of his worn-out boots. Father immediately sat down and took off his boots and insisted that this trooper take them. At first, the young soldier didn't want to take the "padre's" boots, but he soon learned how persuasive our "Sky Pilot" was when he decided it was the right thing. I'm sure it was more than sheer chance that they wore the same size boots!

Our padre was the type of man who was absolutely dedicated to his life as a priest of God. He never lost faith nor seemed to fear physical danger or death. In the world of mortal combat, men pay little attention to words but always notice actions driven by loyalty and courage, especially when it's done with humility.

So it was with Father Bob; he was soft-spoken, never pushy, for he admired and loved "his boys" too much to constantly preach to them. He skillfully guided and led their spiritual journey in a quiet, Christlike way. The essence of Father Gariepy was personified that Sunday as he stood stone-still and totally calm as four Russian 122 mm rockets came in during our Mass in camp. I can still see him standing with the sacred host in his hand as shrapnel dust and dirt showered around and on our canvas church. In a split second, all of us were diving for the dirt floor, but Father calmly asked, no one in particular, "Was that incoming?"

Photo 7: Rockets hit Camp Evans

Photo 8: Aid station area

The Enemy Within

One day, several of us medics were choppered into a battle site where one of our units was badly mauled.

We were met with a muggy stillness typical of the dense jungle that was a big part of the life of a grunt! Wounded and dead were scattered in the area where the fight had erupted. There were men in need of medical care but a shortage of medics.

From the first moment I walked into this particular mass casualty situation, I knew these brave troopers had been through pure hell! With dead and wounded strewn throughout the area, there was no lack of need for urgent medical care. The first soldier who caught my eye had multiple fragment wounds and was near shock. I immediately ran to him and worked to seal off his chest wound. With a "sucking" chest wound, we used the plastic off our wound badges to seal the entrance and exit wound to keep the lungs from collapsing from outside air pressure.

As I worked intently, I became aware of the soldier sitting next to a dead man trying to get my attention. As I busied myself with plugging bleeding wounds, I blocked out the terrible carnage around me and focused all my attention on the wounded man in front of me. However, I felt the empty stare of the young sergeant sitting next to the dead man, doggedly watching me. We medics had long become used to reading our brothers' eyes and hearts as we tried to comfort and ease their suffering bodies.

"Doc, you know what this ****** did to me?" After several attempts to get my full attention, I finally said, "No, what did he do?" He replied, "This is my very best friend. He was the one that kept me going in this insane hell; when I couldn't stand another second of this shit, he was there to keep me going, with words of hope and off-the-wall bullshit to let me know he was here with me, and together we can make it."

As I cleaned and bound up my patient's perforated chest, the young sergeant seemed determined to talk to me about this terrible battle. After several tries of, "Hey, Doc, you know what this no-good b****** did to me?" I finally turned some of my focus to him and said, "No, what did he do?"

With a faraway, detached look, he calmly told his story. "After this firefight, we were sitting here having a cigarette when he pulled up his 45 and dropped the safety as he asked me if I wanted to die. I said, 'Not particularly,' when he said, 'Well, I do!' He put the pistol to the side of his head and pulled the trigger!" As he was telling me this, I was looking at the dead man whom I had already been aware of as I had walked up to them a few minutes earlier. He had a massive head wound, which had left no doubt there was no life left. The left side of his head had been blown away. "This was my very best friend in the world. He was all that was keeping me going in this sorry-assed world, and that no-good ***** blew his brains out right in front of me and left me in this hell! And how in the hell am I supposed to make it now?!" I had no answer, only deep, soul-wrenching love and compassion for him as I looked into his eyes. I hope he felt my compassion for him, but there are no words in our spoken world worthy of this kind of grief.

Many times in the past fifty-some years, I thought of him and prayed he had found someone or some way to make it the rest of his tour, and then the "big one," the rest of his life. How can these grunts possibly fit into the soft, self-centered world that was all they had to come home to? Who are they going to tell their story to? Who is going to care enough to even want to know? Hardly a day has gone by when I didn't offer a fervent prayer to Our Lord for him and his best buddy, but in my heart, I'm afraid he, too, died but not as quickly as his brother, but a slow, painful death, with many long, terrifying nights. The longest-lasting casualties of war are the survivors!

I'm so very sorry, brother. ~Doc

Ragen

The siren was wailing its warning across the hilltop as the ker-rump…ker-rump of the mortars confirmed the alert. It was a little after two in the morning, and VC mortars were on schedule. Everyone in the sand-bagged tents were scrambling for the bunker just forty feet away. We all had our steel "pots," flak jackets, weapons, and ammo within seconds and were funneling into the main aisle of the tent, past the foot of the twenty-some oak and canvas cots. All of us, that is, but Ragen. Ragen did not handle all this very well, and so he stayed pretty well out of it at night, with lots of cheap Korean beer (Oriental Brew). This particular night, he was past the talking stage, and as I ran by his bunk, being second or third to last out, I found him hanging across his cot, head and feet one direction and his air mattress and poncho in the other.

"Ragen, Ragen, incoming…incoming…. We're getting mortared. Get your ass up and get your flak jacket, helmet, rifle, and hit the bunker!" As I'm shaking the hell out of him, I only get a garbled mumble out of him. He's not only unaware of the danger but simply wanted me to leave him alone. I immediately realized that this would not get the job done, so with a yank on his shoulder, I easily rolled his limp body off the low bunk, onto the dirt floor, and threw him snuggly against the sandbag wall. I covered his chest and neck with his flak jacket and put his head in his helmet while yelling to him to stay put: "Don't get up, don't go outside!" I heard the mortars exploding off the side of the hill, each getting louder and closer!

In only a minute or two, all medics and our three doctors, Father Gariepy (our Catholic chaplain), and all the wounded men we had kept for the night were down in the large underground 30- by 30-foot bunker. Our bunker was the best on the hill; those "great" combat engineers always took good care of the aid station. They had done a first-class job making it extra heavy duty, with massive 12x12 wooden beams overhead covered with heavy metal aircraft landing pad material and about two-and-a-half to three feet of sand bags on top of the walls. As good as this bunker was—we knew it had stopped the mortars from past attacks—we were not so sure about the 122 mm Russian rockets they were throwing at us now.

We all poured down the six or seven neatly cut steps to fill the whole area in the dark, musty bunker, hoping it would be the other guy who stepped on or crowded those keen-eyed little critters down there! As soon as everyone was in and settled, Major MacDonald began calling out the names of all under his command, including all the medics, the other doctors, and of course, our "Sky Pilot." As his list whittled down our numbers, I was desperately trying to decide whether to answer for Ragen or to let his lot fall where it may. As the Major called out, "Ragen... Ragen... where in the hell is Ragen??" I felt he deserved an explanation, so I said, "Sir, he's asleep in our tent. I couldn't get him up, so I pushed him against the sandbags and covered him with his flak jacket and helmet." There was a long tense silence with the only sounds coming from outside—the siren and the exploding mortars. Being near the opening, I could see the Major's silhouette from the flash of light sent by the exploding mortars. He was standing with one foot on the lower step, his right arm up and appearing to hold up the bunker as he leaned against the framed opening. He was mumbling a few choice words as he shook his head in disgust. We were a close family out here in the forward aid station, and we all knew how the Major, and each of us, felt for one another. It was tough for each of us dealing with all the misery, pain, suffering, and death that we saw daily. We helped each other in any way we could, without losing our own stability. Major "Mac" had the toughest job! He was a fine, caring doctor like our other two, plus a man in command, thus responsible for our safety, well-being, and actions.

Some of the pressure was taken off the moment as the clatter of an M-16 rifle bounced off something and rattled to the mud floor. By the choice words and comments that slashed out into the darkness, it became obvious that someone's careless handling of their weapon resulted in a battered skull.

Standing near the bunker opening, I could see out and across to our tent. All the while, I hoped that Ragen would just stay put long enough for the all-clear signal. Ragen was a few years older than the rest of us (actually about ten or more), so taking into account the weakening of bladder control and amount of beer he had consumed, I knew the odds were stacked against him staying put!

Sure as hell!! The flap slowly slid back and a somewhat unsteady arm appeared, followed by a crumpled figure. Even in the spaced flashes of light, I saw the tension and fear on his face as he moved slowly out into the darkness. I almost expected him to freeze in his tracks as Major Mac's head turned toward him, and his face took on a granite profile as his jaw tightened! The one thing I hadn't even thought of was his giant, dry cell super flashlight. The loud click of the switch as the bright narrow beam of light shot off the top of the hill still rings in my memory! Ragen, being the careful guy that he was, was not satisfied with simply lighting the way; he had to check out every corner and shadow as he inched his way to the john. The tension was building as he crept along, swinging his powerful light from side to side, up and down, recklessly throwing a long beam of white light into the endless darkness. I watched the Major's body become more rigid as Ragen's steps brought him closer. Somehow, I just knew he couldn't possibly sneak by such a deep dark pit as our bunker without checking it out carefully.

The first beam of light hit the Major square in the face, zapping his "night vision" and illuminating his stern face! The beam of light wavered across his face, hesitating here and there as if to confirm he really was seeing what his eyes were telling him. It traveled down the length of his jungle fatigues, jumping from side to side. The beam swung past Major Mac and jumped from face to face, illuminating from the dark hole a variety of military people. His light pointed out young aggressive, "hard-hitting" medics who could handle any medical crisis, it pointed out our other two doctors, Doctor Klein and Doctor Jamenez, whose hands were "pure magic" and whose quick assessment and delegation of medical procedures had saved many a young, torn body! Just for a moment, I also saw the faces of some of those young, bandaged warriors, but then in another fraction of a second, they were gone…

55

After the light danced randomly around and across the ceiling, it jumped back out the doorway. It swung from side to side again as Ragen continued down the slight slope toward the screened-in "two-holer." Every couple of steps, the light would jump out at a right angle as if to catch someone closing in on his flanks!

I often wonder what the VC thought as they dropped mortar after mortar on us that morning. It had to be "some kind of Capitalist trick to throw off their aim." The Major stood through the forty-five-minute attack, almost casually watching as Ragen stumbled back to his bunk with sporadic mortar explosions in the area. His trip to the outhouse in the middle of a mortar attack left us all speechless. I mean, what could we say?

Photo 9: Bunker we used with wounded where Regan was flashing the light inside.

Another Day in Vietnam

There are few times in our lives when we find someone we can actually bare our soul to. When it happens, it truly is a joyous thing to the soul.

It was our first night on Hill 63, LZ Baldy, a few days after the start of the Tet Offensive, 1968. We had spent most of the afternoon unloading trucks filled with our aid station tents, generators, and medical supplies.

As evening fell, we—the medics and doctors along with a handful of combat engineers who were helping us move from Hill 35, just north of Chu Lai—began to look for shelter underground. At the site of the soon-to-be aid station, there was a partially collapsed underground bunker, to which we found a small opening. The bunker and surrounding hill had been blown up pretty good by VC mortars while the marines were there. So, we inherited the area after they had worked it over with a number of HE (high-explosive) rounds.

As you entered this underground bunker, you noticed what once had been a pretty decent layout. A couple bunks had been built into the walls with an odd assortment of crude but functional pieces of furniture. The marines who had lived here appeared to have been ingenious builders, with what little they had to work with.

That first night down in that dark, dank bunker, with only a couple candles to see by, I struck up a conversation with one of the combat engineers. It all began when he noticed I was eating my C rations cold and came over to where I was sitting on one of the bunks to offer me a piece of C-4. We used C-4 (a plastic explosive) to cook with; it would burn about 3000 degrees Fahrenheit, producing a tall blue flame. The piece he was offering me was about the size of the end of your thumb. It was rounded and smudged from having been carried for a length of time. Since it was hard to come by, I asked him if it was all he had for himself. He said, "Yes, but you use it, Doc. I won't need it." After a couple of gentle nudges to use it, I put it down on the mud floor, placing it between three small stones, and proceeded to open several cans of the Cs I wanted to heat. After insisting he share my humble hot meal, we settled back into conversation. As we talked, the VC dropped mortars on our hill. It was more to let us know they knew exactly where we were and that they could hit us whenever they wanted rather than to get us. I clearly remember the distinctive ker-rump…ker-rump of the mortars and the slight tremor of the earth. As we talked into the darkness, my soul felt lighter, and I had the distinct impression that it was the same for him.

He was a rather tall, blond young man (as we were all young then) with a "salt of the earth" upbringing. We had a lot in common, coming from similar backgrounds. He was a farm boy from Iowa. But still, there was something different and special about our trust in each other and our enthusiasm to share our points of view and philosophy on life itself.

When you live eyeball to eyeball with death, and it's as real as the sun in the morning, you tend to cut through the formalities and protocol you've grown up with and just talk straight, honest feelings. So it was with this young soldier and me. We talked on into the early morning hours, touching on subjects close to our hearts and far from the ears of our own families and friends. It's hard to remember all the things we discussed, but for me, it was as if I had known him most of my life.

Finally, after resting through the last few morning hours, I was up with the rest of the medics and doctors preparing for the inevitable flow of combat casualties by throwing up several tents so that we would have some kind of shelter for the wounded when the Dustoff medevac choppers came. Before twilight, my new friend had already gone down off Hill 63 in a five-ton truck to get to Highway One on his way to our supply depot. Combat engineers would be tasked with transporting medical supplies, food, sandbags, and ammo—whatever we needed back at our new site, Hill 63. As the sun was breaking clear and golden across the rice paddies and onto our pock-marked hill, we already had one Dustoff in with five casualties. I had just helped bring one in on a litter and was busy cutting away parts of his uniform and boot laces when several body bags arrived on a two-and-a-half-ton truck. As I was bent over the wounded grunt working on his wounds, one of the combat engineers working with us tapped me on the shoulder. As I turned to see what was needed, he was motioning with his thumb toward the body bags. "Hey, Doc, your buddy you were talking with last night hit a land mine on Highway One about an hour ago. He's in one of those body bags."

The combat engineer continued, "Both he and the guy driving the five-ton were under the truck in the rice paddy after the mine rolled it, crushing and drowning them." I'll never forget the controlled impact on my heart as I kept on working on the wounded man, with no more than a side glance toward the bodies. Already the heat from the morning sun caused droplets of sweat to zigzag down my face. I looked to the horizon to the sound of another medevac chopper popping the clear morning air with an urgency all too familiar. Another day had dawned in the war on the "dark side" of the world...

Photo 10: Partially destroyed bunker where we bared our souls.

Hill 35 Death Watch

The cloudy, dreary days on Hill 35 were filled with the dead, dying, and terribly wounded. This particular span of time seemed like one long continuous day and night of roaring choppers blowing dirt and mud into our tents. There were always endless lines of poncho-covered bodies, staggering wounded, and traumatic amputations.

One of these many dark (we maintained a blackout condition to discourage VC mortar fire), rainy nights, we had the usual string of assorted casualties, except for one very young soldier. He had been brought to our aid station by some of his newly made buddies from his infantry platoon. He had received mortal wounds from shrapnel to his upper body and was semiconscious. Here was this young boy, probably nineteen but looking sixteen, dying, and we couldn't do any more for him, nor could we get a chopper out to Da Nang. It appeared, as time dragged on, that he was regressing back through his young life, back into his childhood. The whole thing was heartbreaking; in the dim light of the aid station tent, four or five hard-core grunts sat in dark silence, not a dry eye among them. Their buddy cried out in a boyish voice, "Don't leave me, Mommy. I'm sorry, I won't do it again. Please don't leave me, Mommy."

This whole scene continued most of the night, with intermittent outcries from our dying young soldier. All the while, we, the medical staff and his friends, kept vigil with him. Finally, in the early morning hours, all was quiet, and our young soldier faded from this world.

I'll never forget this heartrending drama, infused with a mildew smell mixed with that of canvas and medical supplies. The sight of ragged-bone, tough grunts with a lump in their throats and glistening eyes, keeping watch over this "little brother" of theirs, who had had so little time in combat, so little time to live, yet such loyal friends to stand beside him at his death. I've never witnessed greater love and friendship among grown men, especially among these hard-core infantry soldiers.

Thanks, Marine

Many of our army units in the Americal Division worked shoulder-to-shoulder with U.S. Marine infantry units in I Corps in 1967 and 1968. My unit, the 196th Light Infantry Brigade, was involved in combined combat operations with the marines, which often meant we were involved in medical care for their wounded marines; there was absolutely no difference between the army and marine grunt. The infantry grunt, whether marine or army, was the same brave, tough American that I had come to know well, to respect greatly, and to admire beyond words.

There is no doubt in my experience in the hell of war that the American soldier is the toughest, bravest, most dedicated soldier in the world. They come in all sizes, shapes, ethnic backgrounds, and walks of life. I'll always be the proudest of being accepted as a brother to them and will always be willing to give my all, my very life, for them and consider it a great honor to do so.

On one of those many blazing hot, terrible days of chopper after chopper, loaded with suffering wounded, I found myself working over a torn-up marine. A number of us medics worked frantically trying to stabilize and reassure our wounded men; that particular day, we had a mixture of army and marine casualties. I had just received a clean set of jungle fatigues; when we would get a chance for clean uniforms, it was hit or miss on size. That day, I was one of the last to grab a pair. Having had a busy morning, I ended up with a waist size meant for a man with a little more meat on his hips, so I had a problem—keeping them on.

Somewhere in this organized confusion of triage and carrying our serious casualties to waiting choppers, I mentioned my difficulty keeping my pants up to the medic working next to me. The marine grunt I was preparing to be loaded onto our medevac chopper overheard my comment and started to unbuckle and remove his combat belt. With much effort and struggle, the seriously wounded soldier stripped his marine corps belt from his fatigues. He handed the loose belt up to me and said with a grin, "I figure I have a million-dollar wound" (an injury that would send him home but not in a body bag). I wore that marine belt the rest of my tour in 'Nam and many years on construction jobs since then. It's one of my most valued mementos from the Vietnam War. I still wear it on special occasions and have often prayed he did well in life. I wonder if he ever had any idea how much that simple gesture meant to me on that hot, faraway, forgotten hilltop and how proud I was to accept such a gift of brotherhood from a fellow warrior. For me, it represents the sweat, endurance, hardships, and courage of the American grunt in the Vietnam War.

Our Sky Pilot

In May of 1968, the 196th Light Infantry Brigade had just moved further north near the DMZ. We were operating out of Camp Evans with the 101st Airborne Division, in the A Shau Valley, north of the old capital of South Vietnam, Huế. It was another Sunday, a day like every other in a combat infantry outfit. There was the usual activity preparing to engage the NVA and Viet Cong with weapons preparation, ammo tending, and strategy for the next contact.

It was late on this clear, hot afternoon when I noticed from our aid station tent one of our platoons saddling up to move out into the jungle for a night ambush. They were busy loading their rucks with ammo, C rations, grenades, claymore mines, trip flares, and whatever else they thought necessary. After about thirty minutes of this, they slogged off down the hill heading southwest with the point man and slack man out front and the rest of the thirty-man platoon following single file at five-yard intervals. As each grunt walked by, bent under the weight of his ruck, he had the sober look of men older than their nineteen or twenty years. What was his chance of becoming another of Vietnam's victims? As they headed off into the dense jungle picking their way through our perimeter wire, our "Sky Pilot" came by, obviously preoccupied with another of his own missions.

Our chaplain, Father Bob Gariepy, better known as our "Sky Pilot," seemed to just happen by whenever there was need for a man of God. In this troubled land where men die every day and young soldiers become old in one night, he was busy all the time. When our men were badly wounded or dying, he would be there comforting, praying, and administering Last Rites. Anytime you saw him, he was either coming from or going to one of these "missions of mercy." Whatever the situation, there were inevitably spiritual events happening in men's souls.

As soon as I saw him, I knew I was in for a chance to be a part of one of these experiences, which in itself was stirring since I was no stranger to this man's courage. I was always honored to be along, no matter how "hairy" these missions were.

As I had expected, he asked if I would drive him out in a jeep. (Father always asked even though he wore the rank of captain.) As I hustled to grab a jeep and proceeded to stash my flak jacket, M-16 rifle, ammo, helmet, and web gear, I noticed a curious smile on his face. In due time, after observing my gear preparations, he asked, "What are you doing?" He proceeded to give me a brief rundown on what we were about to do. His plan was to drive a trail parallel to the perimeter for about one mile, then to hump straight out through the jungle to intersect the grunts' line of travel before the sun would set. He must have seen my eyes widen and sensed me mentally saying, "Why wouldn't I bring all this gear along?" Finally, as we climbed into the jeep, he chuckled and said, "Okay, Dave, if it makes you feel better, bring all that stuff along."

After driving about a half mile, I pulled up short to a sign stating, "This trail is mined, has **not** been cleared---Do Not Pass beyond this point." Almost immediately, Father asked why I had stopped. What could I say? Again, he laughed. "If you see any mines on your side, drive around them, and I'll tell you if I see any on my side." After a short pause, he added, "Don't worry, the Lord isn't going to take me now. He knows there are too many boys here that need me." At this statement, a strange calmness came over me and the knot in my stomach was all but gone. I remember thinking, *if it is time for me to die— I cannot find a better man to be with.*

After driving on another half mile, the trail ended. I parked the jeep and prepared to hump the rest of the way. As I was buckling up my gear, again with a tone of curiosity rather than concern, he asked, "*Now* what are you doing?"

I tried to explain the danger of the two of us cutting a trail at dusk through a part of the A Shau Valley in enemy territory, trying to catch up to an infantry platoon, already a half-mile ahead and gaining. Again, he smiled and asked me to have more faith. I was becoming less worried.

65

However, I had been in-country too long to be foolish. I pushed on, trying desperately to be aware of everything in front, around, and behind us. We cut across a small valley and skirted a low ridge. Pushing through dense jungle without using trails is a job for an experienced point man, not this medic. Memories of the difficult time I had finding trip wires and booby traps back in my first week in-country flashed into mind. The ten-day training session covered ambush sights, booby traps with their different types of trip wires, and the ways to conceal them. I was thankful to find out the medics were not walking point in the 196th, and I'm sure the grunts felt the same way. After a tense forty-five minutes picking our way through the jungle, we spotted the platoon digging in on top of a small hill.

As we came up the slope of the hill unannounced, a hush came over the weary grunts, and a subtle look of amazement mixed with bewilderment greeted us. I know they must have thought they had seen everything. A chaplain and a medic strolling out of the jungle like they didn't have a care in the world. This in itself got their attention. I busied myself with one of the grunt's foxholes, one that was a little deeper than the rest, and was starting to level the dirt pile a little for the altar cloth for Mass when Father stilled my hand. I realized later that this is the way he was; he never wanted to do anything that might antagonize any of "his boys." He then set up his altar vessels on top of the altar cloth that covered the small mound of loose dirt. As I assisted him with Mass, I recalled fond memories of my boyhood back in the "world," when being an altar boy was very much a part of my simple protected life in a small Kansas Catholic farm community.

This Mass was one of the most inspiring points in my life. There was a quiet over the hill. Most all the men stopped whatever they were doing and either knelt or squatted out of respect. Even those who knew little of the Catholic service showed a reverence that was truly admirable. The talking and foul language was down to a few whispers. It was obvious that this "melting pot" of tough American grunts was truly taken by this "fearless" man of God.

In the short thirty minutes of the service, I had a chance to study a number of faces. I saw young men with creases and lines on their weathered faces that their friends back home didn't have. I saw eyes that had seen too much too soon, faces that looked extremely tired from endless humps and constant stress. I saw faces that had that familiar "1000-yard" stare from watching friends and fellow grunts blown and shot apart, but desperately trying to hang onto their young, precious lives.

After Father's words of encouragement and warm greetings to each of the men, they crowded around him, asking with the respect of inspired children for any religious articles Father might have. Most of them knew he always carried a number of these and was quite happy to give them away. I saw soldiers with small crucifixes stuck in their helmet bands, rosaries around their necks, and small copies of the New Testament bulging from the top pocket of their jungle fatigues.

As we left that hill, the sunny Sunday turned to a golden twilight. On the faces of these men, I saw hope, respect, and even love for this man, this chaplain who, without any earthly concern for his own safety, found these boys, these grunts, so important that he walked through the jungles (many times) of this dangerous country to be with them, to give them spiritual strength in their most desperate hours.

The American infantry soldier of Vietnam paid little attention to words but noticed sincerity and fearlessness created by deeds. I was truly honored to be standing in the shadow of this man, our "Sky Pilot."

Photo 11: Catholic church Father Gariepy dedicateted

Photo 12: The Sky Pilot's Jeep

Photo 13: Father Gariepy giving 1st Platoon C Co. communion on Hill 348 (Also see front cover photo)

Photo 14: Father Gariepy and Dave Hilger

Gut Feelings – Larry's Story

The night ambush squad of eleven marines moved out, skirting the raised paddy dike with Larry on point. The moon was full with few clouds, so Larry knew he would have to be especially careful about silhouetting the men. Staying to the shadows, he carefully threaded his way into the jungle, heading to the river where their ambush was planned. Larry, being an experienced and careful point man, was cutting his way through, never using a trail where the going is much easier but much more likely to be booby-trapped. The VC (Viet Cong) were cunning and ingenious in the ways they set booby traps to kill and maim our troops. For starters, needle-sharp punji sticks (sharpened bamboo slivers fired to make them tough as steel) were set in a hole, foot-sized to man-sized, with four- or five-foot spikes. These punji stakes either had manure or snake venom on them to make the anticipated wound nasty and/or deadly. The VC were also good at trip wires, often hooked to a grenade or claymore, and many times wired to a second explosive back down the trail. These secondary booby traps were many times set in a tree over the trail configured to blow down (instead of "blowing up") to kill many more of our men.

A point man was of a special breed of men. They were selected by the platoon leader (the lieutenant) with the approval and careful training of the current experienced point man. Oftentimes, they walked point with the "old-timer" for a number of weeks until he, the experienced guy, felt the new guy was ready to go it on his own. The pressure, responsibility, and stress are hard to imagine when he was literally guiding the men into a deadly environment where he was calling the shots on their very lives.

Knowing all this, Larry was extra alert this night, trying to imagine the fear of a trip wire in the dark. Staying in the shadows of the jungle paralleling the river and advancing very slowly, Larry put the men down with a slow hand signal. As the squad leader edged his way toward Larry, he was warned that there was movement across the river. The squad leader signaled the men to stay low and quiet as he softly discussed the situation with the point man.

The shadowy figures of unknown identity slowly became more distinct as they entered the river. They were silhouetted by the light of the rising moon. Larry explained his gut feelings: "There's something wrong here. The helmets don't look right, and the figures are too tall." Larry's squad set up in a line along the edge of the trees, aware and ready, a mere 50 or 60 yards away from the shadows. They watched as each of the figures pulled themselves up and out of the river. As they fell into a line about two yards apart, walking parallel to the water of the river, they made perfect targets for the marine squad's marksmen. They let them all come out of the river, holding their fire, allowing each of the thirteen men to enter the squad's "kill zone."

Carefully watching each man across the river as their outlines were exposed, the squad leader agreed with his point man that it just doesn't look right. "We'll let them go." He signaled the squad not to fire. After waiting long enough to be sure the figures were well out of range to detect their own squad's movement, the marines moved on to their planned ambush site. It was a long night of each man wondering and going over the encounter over and over in his mind, trying to decide if they had let the enemy go, and thus will possibly face them again, this time with those shadowy figures watching and waiting for *their* squad.

The ambush was uneventful and long as usual, enduring mosquitoes, strange sounds, and movement in the shadows, making the soldiers tense and tired from the stress of being on high alert. Later, they found out that another one of their marine units had a squad lost—lost in Larry's squad's area of operation!

As long as I experience life and find people I admire, the point men I knew and watched operate in the jungle of Vietnam will always be top of my list. These young men (most nineteen or twenty years old) shouldered responsibilities that would boggle the minds of our citizens in our safe world here in the United States.

Jay's Story

In May of 1968 the 196th moved north near the DMZ into Camp Evans and operated in the A Shau Valley. (This was the area where the "Hamburger Hill" battle took place in 1969!) We were sharing Camp Evans with the 101st Airborne Division. As soon as our aid station was set up we were busy with combat casualties. This area was well known to be a "hot" area for the grunts that operated in it.

It was among those 101st troopers that I was honored to eventually become a friend to Jay Goodrich who was from, of all places, Wichita, Kansas! We were both on Camp Evans at the same time, however I didn't know him until many years later at a Vietnam Veteran's reunion. It was at that time he related an amazing personal encounter with a Viet Cong soldier in the A Shau Valley.

It was at the end of a long all-day search and destroy mission. His company was preparing a night perimeter. Whenever we prepared a place to stay for the night there were men posted out around the area to provide security while the main body of grunts dug in and had a chance to eat their C's (C-rations). Jay was positioned on a trail where he sat on his ruck with his M-16 rifle across his legs eating his C's. Soldiers on these S & D missions stayed alive by always being alert and aware of their surroundings and anyone unexpectedly coming into their survival zone.

In the jungle of Vietnam things happened quickly and at close range! As Jay sat alert, a Viet Cong soldier stepped around a bend in the trail, suddenly appearing about thirty meters in front of Jay. Jay said he knew immediately that the Viet Cong had him! The V.C.'s AK-47 was slung across his chest and he had his right hand on the pistol grip with his finger on the trigger. They both stared intensely into each other's eyes. Jay said he calculated he would lose in a shootout-- all the Viet Cong had to do was pull his rifle around and fire, while Jay would have to grab his M-16 from off his lap, swing it around, hit the safety switch, then fire.

After a very long minute of, as Jay related the sensation, communicating with their minds, Jay got the message loud and clear from the mind of the Viet Cong soldier, "If you don't go for it, I won't go for it." The perhaps one minute these two soldiers faced each other in this decision-making standoff seemed like five minutes to Jay. Then the enemy soldier did an amazing thing. He turned his back on Jay and took two or three slow steps back around the bend, disappearing into the jungle.

Even though Jay's soldierly training might have demanded he shoot to kill the Viet Cong man even as the enemy turned to walk away, Jay admitted, "I had no desire to kill this man!"

These are the good and decent men that I knew and served with. Jay died a few years ago from lung cancer, too many cigarettes, too many hard days and nights trying to forget. Jay, you'll always be a hero to me and a perfect example of the men that fought and died in that war that nobody wanted to remember.

PART THREE:
FIGHTING FOR SURVIVAL

Booby Trap

He was thrashing on the jungle floor, screaming over and over, "I'm going to die!... I'm going to die!......Oh, sweet Jesus, I'm going to die!" As I ran up to him, one quick glance told me that it had been a "Bouncing Betty," and it had done its work exactly as it was designed to do. The young grunt in agony on the ground had both legs shredded from the knees down, and two men behind him had died instantly, as red hot chunks of steel slashed into their chests and throats. They had been blown back and were lying crumpled and broken in large pools of dark red blood. Even in the dark, still smoking jungle, I knew these two had finished their time in hell. After a quick examination to confirm what my eyes and experience had told me, I was on the man who was still crying for our help with his desperate words of despair.

In times like these, instinct training and many prayers for guidance seemed to take control. The mind became solid and very clear in its control of the body. Everything I knew about survival in this "green hell" caused me to land in the middle of his chest. I grabbed two fists full of jungle shirt, jerking him up and slamming him down repeatedly on the trail. As my physical attack got his attention, I yelled in his face, "That's a hell of a way to talk! You're not going to die! You're not going to die!" After three or four hard slams on his back, he settled down enough for me to work on his wounds.

The left leg from the knee down was gone, except for a narrow strip of burnt flesh that held his boot behind him, still laced around his foot. The shiny white tibia jutted out. The right leg was split from the knee down to the top of his boot, lying open like a gutted, burnt fish. There was very little blood; the terrible heat from the flash of the mine had seared the flesh, cauterizing blood vessels to the point of almost stopping the flow of blood. I stabbed a syrette (single dose of morphine) into his right thigh, injecting a quarter grain of numbness into his already stunned body.

Got to keep him talking…can't let him go into shock…must keep him fighting

78

hard… Got his web belt pulled up tight above the knee of his left leg, just for added safety…can't let the artery blow, draining blood away…that would surely put him into shock.

"Doc, just tell me which leg is worse." Without hesitation and in my coolest manner, I said, "Your left leg is gone at the knee, the right one is torn up pretty bad; but with modern medical technology, there's a good chance they can put it back together." In my heart, I felt they were both lost, but I had to give him a piece of "hope" with which to start his long road back to the "world."

The landing zone was cleared and secured, the Dustoff medevac chopper was down and waiting with its great rotor pushing the grass and bushes aside. The blast of hot air was welcome in that stagnant greenhouse, where the heavy, sticky air of the jungle hung on us like our sweat-soaked jungle fatigues. We ran toward the chopper, carrying him in his own poncho, with both boots at odd angles. The roar of the turbine engine and the rush of air by my head made it hard to hear his words. I held onto his hand, telling him he was on the way, "You're going back to the world…hang in there and never give up!"

"Thanks, Doc. I know what you did for me… Thanks, Doc…you take care, Doc… God bless you, Doc!" He would ride back beside his dead friends already getting cold to study the insanity of war and begin his personal torment that would last for the rest of his life… *Why me?* (Not so much as why his legs, but why he was still alive.)

The chopper lifted straight up, up, up, over the sixty-foot trees, swung around, dipped its nose, and roared away. I watched as the white cross on its belly faded into the green jungle and listened to the whine of the engine until, after a minute or two, the jungle was quiet again.

Dear Lord, look after this young soldier, who now begins the longest and hardest "hump" of the rest of his life. Help him, Lord, first to keep fighting to stay alive in the next few months and then to accept his cross back in the world where no one will care long enough for him to unburden his soul. And that in each stage of his suffering and healing, there will be someone to hold his hand, to encourage him and urge him on when there is nothing to go on for. Guide him to your side, Lord, when this trivial world, with all its hollow pleasures, has become a dark vacuum of nothingness! Let him feel Your hands on his torn bleeding soul when he cries out to a deaf world, and when the "best buddies" and "Docs" are all gone! Amen.

No One Exempt

Standing over the young Air Force pilot who had just bailed out of his now destroyed burning fighter jet, I was struck by his spit-shined boots. He was too strange in this world of gray weeping sky, mud, filth, and hopeless drudgery. Where did this American warrior come from? I had forgotten that men lived in a place where shined boots, clean uniforms, shaved faces crowned with a neat, fresh haircut were the status quo. And yet he had left all that to die trying to save us, the "mud crunchers," the "ground pounders," the "grunts" who are the point of the spear of ground combat.

"Punching out" of his stricken jet after a devastating air strike, he had hit the rice paddy with no parachute deployed. It's unbelievable what the human body can withstand and remain intact. The speed and force at which he had hit the ground was hard to imagine. It was far beyond terminal velocity, for his upper chest was noticeably enlarged from the explosive force the impact caused to his internal organs. So peaceful he looked in his clean flight suit with his .38-caliber pistol still strapped in his shoulder holster. My eyes were drawn to his neatly placed gleaming name tag, Capt. _____, which I remember plainly noting and not remembering after he was out of sight. After years of sorting out my many experiences as a medic in the infantry in Vietnam, I realized this was a pattern: I kept dead soldiers impersonal and distant. I have no memory of what this young pilot looked like nor much of anything that happened that afternoon, except the condition of his body.

He had the same look of all the dead men I had seen until we tried to pick him up. Another medic and I were to place him onto a poncho and carry him to a waiting medevac chopper, a Dustoff. I lifted his lower body by gripping his heels as the other medic picked up from his shoulders. As we lifted in unison, we were taken aback to see his body sag oddly as his legs in my hands bowed backward as if made of soft rubber. Despite our grasps on the body's shoulders and feet, most of his body stayed on the rice paddy ground, and we immediately knew we were going to need more

81

help.

It took three of us to raise his body off the ground and get him onto the poncho. I placed my hands under his calves and thighs, and as I lifted, everything between my hands sagged with a grinding noise.

Once again, a journey begins for one of our bravest of the brave who gave his all to save his fellow combat brothers.

Saving Dick Moss

It was my turn to pull bunker guard duty on the perimeter about two hundred yards down the hill from our aid station. As it was monsoon season, it rained almost all the time, turning our compound into a slimy mud environment everywhere we walked.

As medics, we took our turns on bunker guard since everyone appreciated being able to rest at night knowing we had brothers on watch. This particular night, it was raining constantly, and I wasn't real certain my buddy with me could be dependable, so I stayed awake all night until a medic came out to the bunker to relieve me about 2:30 a.m. Major MacDonald, our doctor, wanted me back at the aid station. We had word that there were casualties coming. This night, I could hear the other medics having a good time singing and enjoying the few beers we had been saving. Needless to say, I was feeling a little left out, since my share was sure to be gone by the time I got back.

We got around at night with a combat flashlight with a red lens; it would give you enough light to walk safely and be aware of your immediate surroundings without being seen very far away. As I was plowing through the mud looking forward to getting into my dry tent and maybe having a little rest on my cot before we got busy with the wounded, I was also simply content to be getting back to my job.

As soon as I walked around the short wall blocking the tent opening, I swung my light to my right and saw an empty cot. Since everything had quieted down, the medics were all in their cots. I knew there was nowhere for anyone to be but in their rack! I asked the one guy at the other end of the tent, who was up writing a letter, "Where's Moss??" He gave me some half-hearted answer: "I have no idea. Who made you the mother hen?" At that moment, I felt a great urgency to find Moss, feeling it was life or death. As I started to search, I suddenly and inexplicably "saw," like a video in my mind, him turning right as he approached the tent instead of turning left, which was the way to enter the tent. Turning right would bring him to

83

the outside walk where we had a stacked wall of sandbags to protect our tent from mortars. Thinking he was going inside the tent, he was tripped by the rope holding the tent pole up. He fell between the outside tent wall and the sand bags.

I found him there out cold, face down in running water up to his ears. I immediately jerked him up by the back of his jungle shirt, causing him to expel a volume of water from his nose and mouth, coughing and spitting to be able to breathe. I hauled him into the tent and got him on his cot. Lying face down, I turned his head to the side, checking to see if he was breathing okay. I covered him with his poncho liner and pulled his jungle boots off.

I never told him about this, and I'm sure he did not remember that night. A few weeks later, he was sent out to one of our line companies to serve as a platoon medic. I heard from some of his men in his platoon that he was doing an outstanding job as their medic. He had been out on the line for three or four months when he was KIA. He died a hero saving his men. His death in 'Nam has always laid heavy on my heart, often questioning why I was destined to save him from drowning only to have him die a few months later.

Many years later, after the "safe" world had dulled my memory, I was sitting in church after Mass with Dick Moss consuming my mind and questioning that dark, wet night. Within a few moments, these simple words formed clearly in my mind: "Because he needed that time to get it right."

Photo 15: Sgt. Richard "Dick" Moss

Tet '68 Death Watch

A pair of Chinook choppers raised a huge cloud of dust as they hovered in with large connexes slung under them. These connexes came with their own generator and refrigerator unit attached to the top. They were large, all steel containers about thirty feet long and ten feet wide, primarily used to ship cargo overseas on ships. They were strong, watertight and airtight, making them suitable as large coolers to store, then transport, our dead brothers in. On Hill 63 we were getting so many KIA's daily that we couldn't get them to the rear graves registration in Chu Lai fast enough. These containers were modified especially for our dead troopers. They had shelves on both sides with an aisle down the center.

For a number of days we carried our dead to the front ramp of those containers where men from graves registration prepared the bodies for placement in these cold steel tombs. As one was filled, a Chinook was called in to lift it out, fly it to Chu Lai and return with an empty one. I truly felt sorry for these men assigned to this detail as I watched them work day after day. I hope those wounded we worked on daily weren't aware of these boxes for at the same time we were trying to keep their spark of life going, they still were left within sight of those true heroes with pale faces and blank, far-away stares.

The graves registration men's responsibility was to strip the bodies and body parts, then wash them clean with fire hoses while carefully documenting their body wounds to determine possible cause of death. Finally, the men would place each body, and all the parts that came out of the bush with it, in plastic "body bags." The body, as well as the body bag, was tagged with correct ID before it went in to the connex.

Hearing those gas generators running day and night was not only a constant reminder of our dead brothers, but a foreshadow of the mourning wail of the mothers of our bravest sons, forever our heroes.

"Don't Let Me Die"

Tet, 1968

The nineteen-year-old Black grunt grabbed my right hand with his while clutching the other side of the litter with his left. The power of his grip was crushing my hand as I returned equal pressure, letting him know I was there holding onto him, trying desperately to push some of my life into his suffering body. He had terrible frag wounds to his upper body, which were slowly letting his life drain away.

Dr. Klein and Dr. MacDonald were working frantically, as usual, doing everything humanly possible to stabilize him as we waited for a Dustoff to come in. This was but another case of feeling overwhelmingly guilty for not being the one suffering and dying.

As long as I live in this world of hurt and guilt, I shall not forget his desperate pleading: "Hang onto me Doc…please don't let me die…hang onto me Doc…please hang onto me…don't let me die."

It's too late to ask why. It's too late to wonder where he was or what he was doing when the mortar ripped into his strong, young body. I felt so totally helpless with the job that was thrust upon me the second he reached out and grabbed my hand. How would his dear mother ever have been able to handle these minutes when our lives crossed paths, here in a dirty, dusty, hot tent on a "never-to-be-remembered" hilltop in Vietnam?

The medevac chopper hovered in and slipped sideways to get closer to our open-walled tent. I ran with him, this suffering, badly wounded soldier, my hand locked into his, yelling encouragement, hoping he could hear over the roar of the Dustoff, its engine straining to ready for the imminent takeoff that would quickly fly the wounded soldier to our surgical hospital in Chu Lai. His pleadings for me to hang onto him were even more desperate now as we slid his litter into the belly of the chopper.

Many are the regrets in war, as we struggle on in our own aging bodies, for us survivors…with so many wounded brothers and so few of us medical people to try to save them. As the chopper readied for takeoff, I had to force his hand free of mine. To this moment, as I write this, I can feel his "will" go as my hand left his. It was as if I had cut his lifeline free with my razor-sharp knife. The will to live is very powerful, especially when you are young and still have a life to live. Many times I saw men hang on to life, and when their will to live waned or was lost, they faded away.

In our combat medical training, our trainers stressed over and over that our job was to pull our wounded up to give them some of our will, for psychological shock is very deadly—as I soon learned in my tour.

The Dustoff pilot called back on our radio to tell us he had died en route. His radio transmission fell on a numb silence in our aid station as we kept working on the other wounded. Each of us was feeling the stab of hurt in our hearts for a long moment. But we had to go on…for there can be no rest while the evil of war supplies us with endless numbers of wounded, dying, and ruined young bodies.

Oh Lord, please comfort their wounded souls as they face "the big battle" of the rest of their lives, in a world where our fellow protected Americans do not care as we do here!

Rage

It was hot again and the earth was powder dry on top of this hill, the way it is back in Kansas on the farm in August. The heat was sapping my body of energy and strength, but then, I was twenty-two years old and in good physical shape, so my body was working overtime to cool itself with a constant flow of sweat.

As another Dustoff chopper landed, I was already amid a lashing, swirling fog of dust and heat that caused my eyes to squint automatically. Through this dim world of dirt and grit that is enveloping my sweaty body, I saw several walking wounded struggling off the open chopper, dragging their equipment and rifle the best they could. Immediately I know that the two on the floor of the chopper are KIAs by the absolute lack of movement. The two bodies lay there in skewed, unnatural positions on top of their bloody green ponchos, the common mode of transportation used for dead grunts in the bush.

I was first of the four medics there to get them off, so I helped pull the first KIA out, handing his feet to the second man. As he pulled the poncho and feet out, I supported his limp body with my arms and right knee until I got to his shoulders and head. In order to keep his limp arms within the folds of the poncho, I grabbed a roll of poncho on either side of his head, lifting his heavy lifeless body over a litter on the ground. In haste to get him off the chopper, I had not gotten his body far enough down the litter, so that as I lifted up the two handles on my end, his head dropped over the end edges of the canvas litter, letting his brain slip out, landing on top of my right boot.

No matter how long one works in an environment of a forward combat aid station, there never seems to be an end to the incidents that embed themselves in your heart. Even after months of wartime service as a medic, I was not prepared completely to see a man's brain—containing all his life, his love, heartaches, memories of Mom and Dad, home, and family—lying on my dirty, bloody boot!

I walked slower than usual and very carefully so it wouldn't fall off into the dirt, but at the same time hoping that it would. After only a few steps, gravity and balance took over and it rolled off into the dirt, only to be gobbled up in an instant by a mangy dog who had been unnoticed up until this moment. This was like the final slash to my heart, the one that I could not push back with all the many others. I felt the fire burst inside of me, and a great rage overcame me. After placing the litter in the graves registration tent, I stormed into my tent to get my M-16 rifle. As I slapped the rifle away from the side of my bunk and slammed a round into the chamber, the awful reality of the situation suddenly hit me…the poor, damn dog was starving to death. Who can judge?

Photo 16: Wounded were usually transported by a Dustoff chopper

Photo 17: Mass casualties

Dustoff Down

We heard him coming before we spotted the speck on the horizon. There was no doubt that it was another Dustoff, the rapid popping of the rotor and high rpm of the engine telegraphed the urgency. He came in a straight line heading for our aid station, and at about a hundred and fifty feet up and three hundred meters out, I noticed a flash from the tail boom. An object rocketed straight up and disappeared above the Huey. Within seconds, the chopper became very erratic, swinging from side to side. The pilot did an outstanding job of trying to compensate for loss of control; however, a helicopter with no tail rotor is doomed to a spiral rotation from the powerful torque of the main rotor. At about fifty feet up, the chopper was spinning out of control and going down fast into a flooded rice paddy, a couple hundred feet in front of the aid station. As the Dustoff spiraled in faster the closer it got, the centrifugal force overpowered the wounded men inside the open Huey. I can hardly imagine the terror they felt as they were ripped out of the belly of that helicopter. Surely it was an answer to all the desperate prayers coming from these men that they began flying out at about fifty feet (and not sooner) into a flooded rice paddy. Luckily, the pilot had enough control left to make sure he crashed just short of our camp.

We all felt so helpless as the chopper plowed in, churning and breaking in half as the main rotor slapped hard into the mud in the midst of the struggling wounded, pelting them with mud and water. As the chopper slowly stopped thrashing in its death struggle and rolled halfway onto its broken rotor, we were there. The pilot's door slipped open as he frantically rolled out. We all knew that the Huey had a tendency to explode into a fireball, roasting men in seconds. Again, God's hand was on these men; the chopper never caught on fire, and no one was killed in the crash. We found wounded men slathered in the slimy mud that had literally slid into their faces, cramming their mouths full of mud and slime so that they could not breathe properly. As I dug this muck out of one man's mouth, I was struck by the pitiful plight of these men. They were casualties of combat coming to us with all kinds of wounds, and now, to add insult to injury, they were lying in foul, stagnant sewage. But they did miss eternity's gate by a desperate prayer.

As we dug the mud out of their mouths with our fingers, one of the men told me how after hitting the rice paddy, he tried to shield his face as the big rotor slapped within a foot of his face, pelting him with mud and water that stung like shrapnel. Disoriented and stunned, he was frozen by the fear of moving the wrong way. We carried and helped the wounded walk the several hundred feet to the aid station, where one battered, bandaged, mud-plastered soldier summed up his whole day. He had his helmet in one hand, dragging his M-16 rifle in the other as he came up to the aid station. At about ten feet from our sandbagged tent, he let go. He slammed his helmet into the sandbag wall and let out a string of profanity, letting his M-16 smash into the mud. He told the whole world what he thought of the war, the army, and of his superiors. He said everything that the rest of those poor battered men were too numb, too tired, to put into words. That one soldier's epic outburst seemed to be a collective release of pressure for the rest of the wounded, so insulted by fate's piling on of indignity after the bad luck of being injured. There was a wide assortment of combat wounds, now compounded by strained back and neck muscles and their extremity joints being torn from the violent impact. Several had severe back injuries, which we sent off in another chopper as soon as we could get one in. These men would not have survived so well if it hadn't been for them being young, tough, and having excellent muscle tone. They were all grunts whose lives depended on being physically "tough." And, of course, the soft muck, however filthy, of the rice paddy certainly helped.

Photo 18: The Dustoff that went down

Part Four:
Are You Tough Enough?

Alone in Hell!

This is a story that a brother medic (whom I knew well and trained with as a corpsman at Fort Sam Houston the winter of 1967) told me three days after he miraculously found his way back to our fire support base.

His company was ambushed by a battalion-sized NVA (North Vietnamese Army) unit and cut off from their group. After a valiant stand and tremendous heroism, they were overrun. Overrun is a situation in combat that strikes terror in the toughest warrior's heart. It's when you're outnumbered to the point of no hope of survival and you literally make a "last stand."

Dan told me this terrible day began like most other days, humping and sweating and hacking through the jungle. Like most, that is, until the NVA sprang the ambush. He said they had fire coming from all sides, and a number of small groups of our troopers were cut off in the jungle and surrounded! There was desperate combat throughout the morning until early afternoon when it became hopeless. Most of the troops were dead or wounded, and the remaining fighters were low on ammo. No one was coming to save them. Dan said his M-16 blew up in his hands (probably from mud in the bore), and the men around him decided it was every man for himself. The NVA were coming at them from all directions in the final assault with their AKs at hip height on full automatic, killing every American as they came.

It was at this last moment that he turned and ran about twenty yards to his rear; as he rounded a clump of bushes, he decided in that instant to "play dead." He had the presence of mind to splash some hot sauce (we carried hot sauce whenever available to spice up our C rations) on his forehead and neck, pitch the bottle away, and fall face up with his eyes open. Within seconds, three NVA soldiers were on top of him. It was at this point in his storytelling that Dan paused to take a few moments to collect his composure before he could describe the most horrific experience of his young life. Running terrified, his buddies screamed as they died, firing all around. He hung on to sanity by sheer will to survive; as he lay there, he tried to look calm and dead.

Dan was a tested and proven brave medic who had saved many soldiers and had too often seen dead men, so he knew a dead man would have his eyes open. Looking into the eyes of the NVA who had jammed the muzzle of his AK-47 hard to his forehead with his finger locked on the trigger, he tried to relate to me the raw terror he felt as he tried to pray. All he could manage was a silent scream as he waited for the sledgehammer blow of the .30-caliber bullet ripping through his brain.

His mind running wild, he was certain his heart could be heard as it seemed ready to explode, and he knew his chest was rising and falling as he waited for the inevitable. He was kicked in the head several times so hard he felt he was knocked out for a few moments; several ribs were broken as they stripped him of his watch, wallet, ammo, aid bag, and any other equipment they decided would be useful. He said he continued limply rolling with each blow and had to work hard to stay limp and appear lifeless without any resistances or reaction. As they rolled him over into a stream, he let himself roll in a way that allowed the corner of his mouth and one eye to be out of the water. He hung onto that thin thread of sanity as he watched and heard the brutal killing of the wounded, his buddies. He was absolutely certain there would be a parting shot in the back of his head!

This unbelievable nightmare went on for what seemed to be an eternity, which in reality was ten or fifteen minutes, for combat in the jungle was swift, brutal, winner-take-all, and over. The NVA were very aware our brave troopers had gotten radio transmissions out, and we would be pushing it hard to get to them. Lying in that creek, living his whole life second by second, was terror to the point of snapping. Dan told me it took most of the afternoon to make one finger move. He was locked in a body that would not move. If he moved, the NVA would put a bullet in the back of his head. Even though his conscious mind knew they were long gone, his subconscious would not allow him to move. Hour after hour, he concentrated on moving the little finger on his right hand. Finally, he managed a slight twitch, then full movement in that finger. Slowly he got one finger then another and another, then his hand. In this way, he regained control of his whole body. It was almost sundown when he got up on his feet and stumbled through terrible silence in this nightmare of the shadows of lifeless figures who only hours earlier were his brothers, his family.

Finding two other men who had managed to stay alive, the three cut a trail for the LZ they had operated out of. It took three days of staying alive and evading the enemy. It was the third day when I saw him. I had just helped unload the bodies of the men of Alpha Company the day before; chopper after chopper had lifted up, loaded with the bodies of chopped-up, mutilated men who had made their last stand in hell. Before this day was over, six or seven more men found their way to us; all were in sad shape, in shock, exhausted, and needing medical care, not to mention food and water.

Dan was never the same after this time in battle. He couldn't understand why the NVA didn't pull the trigger! Over all, their company had experienced a terrible slaughter, with many of their troopers mutilated beyond words. The men like Dan who survived that awful day were forever changed and certainly called, I believe, to have a special mission in life.

But what that mission would have been I never found out. Dan and I came out of the field (out of the jungle) and turned in our weapons and gear the same day to go home. It was in September of '68, time to go back to the world, back to a place where we would never feel we belonged. On a trip to St Louis about fifteen years later, I decided to look for Dan in the phone book, knowing his last name. Finding several pages of people with his last name, I just picked an individual name at random to start with. Turns out, it was Dan's father who answered the phone! After introducing myself and asking if he had a son who served in Vietnam, he said "Yes, he is sitting beside me!" I asked if I might talk to Dan. We talked for only a few minutes, and I got the message loud and clear that I was a ghost from his past that he had buried, and he didn't want to talk to me. I knew too much about his hell, and he was afraid I'd dig it up. I never got the chance to tell him I was simply happy to know he was alive and very proud to have known and served with him.

Required: Nerves of Steel

It was a dark, starless night, darker than most nights when the clouds blanket the jungle. More of our Dustoffs were coming in, using their landing lights only on the last hundred feet or so. They didn't want to give away our position to the enemy. The men we were dragging off, or lending a shoulder to, were the survivors of an "overrun" position. They had been infiltrated by the VC (Viet Cong) in most of the dark hours, where it was each man for himself. It was among these battered, dazed casualties that I found a bloody, lost young soldier. My heart reached out to him immediately, mainly, I guess, because he had a strong resemblance to my youngest brother, Steve. He had the same blond hair and that innocent, boyish face, and he looked like he hadn't even started to shave. He appeared to be in shock, and with one of the most lost looks I'd ever seen, he kept asking me where he was. His hair was caked with mud and blood, his face and hands the same, all the way down to his boots. I immediately felt his pain and need for a friend but, quickly checking him out, found no physical wounds on him.

He was following me closely with his eyes, asking me over and over why I was concerning myself with him. I told him I was a medic, and that brought a little life to his eyes, as he told me he was a medic also. At this point, I did the only thing I could for him—I listened to him as I wiped his face and hands clean of the mud and blood. This seemed to overwhelm him, as he started to open up to me. "Doc, you won't believe what I had to do tonight." The VC had crawled up to, and into, their night perimeter. The killing went on all night at point-blank range. Our men were firing and fired upon by prone figures moving on all sides, grenades exploding everywhere, and no one able to tell for certain who was friend or enemy. He said as the night dragged on that the VC would toss a rock at a still body, and if it moved, they'd follow with a grenade. He was crawling in the blackness, too scared to think, when he came to a foxhole, and as he eased over the edge, he instantly knew that there was an enemy lying at the bottom. With lightning reflexes, he went in with his razor-sharp knife. (We all carried good heavy sharp knives, especially the medics.) He couldn't remember much after that, except that he held the enemy down as he thrashed with his jugular spurting blood everywhere, even in his mouth. As his nightmare wore on, he had to kill another VC as he came into the hole, silhouetted by the flash of a grenade. The last hours were spent in that shallow hole with two dead, bloody, enemy soldiers smothering him with the strong smell of blood in a slimy pit made from large pools of their blood mixed with their soil. He verified his nightmare by drawing his knife to show me the dried, caked blood and hair plastered to its length, as well as his scabbard on his right hip and leg.

I was so deeply touched by this boy's heartache that I told him to stay put while I left to grab my extra set of jungle fatigues and pair of size 8½ narrow jungle boots I had been hoarding. Everything fit as if I had been holding it for his arrival. I slowly walked with him, as I braced his arm, to the waiting Dustoff that took our worst casualties on to Da Nang. He looked totally lost and disoriented. I think he wasn't even sure if he was still alive. This boy has been in my thoughts and prayers many times since we came home. I can only hope that there was someone else to help him at the next stop on his long journey back…

Rotting Wounds

As soon as I got to the two wounded troopers, I immediately noticed the strong odor of rotting flesh. After stripping these tough grunts of their jungle shirts, it was quite obvious their wounds were at least three days old, each showing advanced stages of decomposing flesh around the edges of the wounds. This was the first time I had seen wounds of this type on a live soldier. The most obvious thing I noticed other than the rancid smell was the enlargement of the entrance wound in a circular oval pattern. As I scrubbed these frag wounds with surgical soap, I remember thinking that there must be more dead soldiers nearby, judging by the smell of the area.

As I continued to clean these wounds, I began to realize the smell was coming from these two men because as the surgical soap entered the wounds, maggots began crawling out. It didn't take long to realize these maggots had been eating away the dead flesh, thus preventing a deadly infection, or at least temporarily buying them time for us to get them out and into our surgical hospital in Chu Lai.

I still remember the toughness of these brave men as one calmly smoked a cigarette and calmly stated as he watched the maggots crawl out of his body, "I knew those bastards were in there; I could feel them moving around."

Civilization Suspended

In December 1967, our medics were on Hill 35. Our aid station wasn't much to look at but was quite efficient and functional. Its center of activity was the main aid tent, a large tent, twenty by thirty-five feet. It was olive drab green with a ten-foot-square panel across the top with a large red cross beaming from a white background. This panel was for our medevac helicopters, helping them to locate us from the air. It was also an aiming point, a target, for Viet Cong mortars and 122 mm Russian rockets.

A little back of the aid tent and to one side were several similar tents we used for our living quarters. These two tents were furnished with two rows of wooden and canvas cots on a dirt floor, most sporting a real luxury, a mosquito net.

The aid tent and the two tents we used for sleeping quarters were to be sandbagged about five feet high all around the exterior walls with a short wall the same height two feet out in front of the openings. This was done so that a near miss by a mortar or rocket would not allow hot slivers of steel to slash through the tent doorway. A round inside the tent would be deadly for anyone in it.

I was taking a short break from the never-ending job of sandbagging these walls. While leaning against the neatly squared end of the door opening, I saw three growing specks on the blue horizon. I tore through the flap as the whop, whop, whop of the three Huey Dustoff choppers announced their high-speed arrival carrying more of our men. I was followed out to the small muddy helipad by two "new" medics running at my heels. They had no idea what to expect, but then that's routine for a forward medical aid station.

The three choppers presented a foreboding sight from a long way off. As they came in hard, with their noses down and their big rotors flexed up from pulling all the air they could, the sight and smell of death blanketed our little hill.

What I saw next shocked me, and I was one of the "old-timers" (after all of three months in-country) on the hill. I knew that these two new medics were about to experience something they would never be able to shake out of their minds. The first thing that I saw, just a moment before the odor of death hit, was a number of rigid arms and legs extending from the open doors on the choppers. From this point on, my world that day seemed to spin down to a numbing slow motion.

As the Dustoffs flared in, one, two, three, in a swirling cloud of choking wet dust, the combination of the sight and smell hit me like a man's fist into my stomach. Just as the last of the three settled on their frail-looking runners, I lost both new medics. They froze like pale pillars of salt. The medic to my right slowed, turned, and heaved his guts out!

The roar of the powerful turbojet engines almost drowned out the first pilot's repetitive scream to "get them the hell off my chopper." I charged, head down, into the lashing downwash of air into and on top of the two-foot layer of dead American grunts.

The choppers were piled full of torn human carnage—beyond description, already rigid with rigor mortis. As I started pulling bodies to the door and out onto the ground, I was repeating over and over in my mind, *"Dear God, I hope these boys can forgive me."* There was no place for my jungle boots but on the different parts of their anatomy. As my mind groped with this hellish reality, I started focusing on details. These brave men were a mixture of Caucasian, black, and Mexican-American heritage, all twisted and interlaced in a mass of cold, stiff brotherhood. Some were missing parts of their body, and some were badly ripped and terribly mutilated by the inhumane hate of the enemy.

As the minutes of handling these brave grunts dragged into hours of slow-motion drudgery, I had to frantically search the choppers' smeared aluminum floors for heads, parts of limbs, and bloody blobs of internal organs.

These men were part of one of our infantry companies that had been cut off, surrounded, and overrun by a large force of North Vietnamese Army troops. To see what they had done to our men would be to understand how ruthless and cruel they were. Our men had been mutilated and brutally tortured as they called out for help. Many had massive damage to the skull from having been shot through the head with their own issue .45-caliber pistols. This battle must have been a terrible, hellish nightmare those last desperate hours. Later I saw some of the survivors, and they appeared to be partially dead inside, just by the "1000-yard" stare they carried in their eyes.

The Mission and Teamwork: Search and Destroy

The Second Platoon leader, a square-faced second lieutenant, came up to me with an unusual air of gentleness and respect. (I was currently assigned to the First Platoon, C Company 3/21, 196th Light Infantry.) He sat on some washed-out sandbags near me as I worked on my aid bag. The standard-issue aid bag held smaller accessories such as tubes of ointment, safety pins, casualty tags, small combat dressings, morphine syrettes, a small surgical kit, and endotracheal tubes. I was packing larger, bulkier dressings, extra cravats, small wire splints, bottles of salt tabs, anti-malaria pills, and water purification tablets in a claymore mine bag (a canvas bag with a long shoulder strap). His tanned, weathered face squinted against the late sun as the last of its rays shot off the top of a nearby mountain range. I glanced up several times, studying his face for clues as to what he had on his mind. He certainly didn't look like he was twenty-three years old. There was an "old man" seriousness in his eyes, the kind that comes with the heavy responsibility of commanding men daily in life-and-death situations.

He sat contented for several minutes. I guess he was studying me also. When he did finally speak, it was as a friend who needs a favor but isn't quite sure how to ask. I knew about what he had in mind. I belonged to the First Platoon, and we had just come in off an all-day S&D (search and destroy). In an infantry company, there are four platoons, and in C Company, the third of the 21st, two platoons would go out while the other two, along with the mortar team, would hold the hill from the enemy. The first and third had been out while his, the second, along with the fourth, stayed on the hill (Hill 348) that day. Since his medic had been wounded and "medevaced" out, he asked if I would go with his platoon the next morning. The gentleness and almost kind way that he asked was touching, since by military regimentation, he could have ordered me to do it, and that would have been that! The mutual respect that we gave each other in "the boonies" was part of our way out of "hell." This was so for each of us: grunts, medics, and officers alike. Of course, I said I would go out with them. I was fairly new with the First Platoon, so I was deeply touched when several of them got a little upset when they heard I would be going out with the Second. Chuck and Monk took me in when I first came to them, starting a lifelong friendship. Both Monk and Chuck as seasoned combat veterans knew the importance of helping the "new guy." A new guy's chances for survival were less than favorable in the jungle unless an old-timer (a man who had survived several "firefights") took him under his wing. They took it seriously when they knew I'd be going back out into the valley the next morning with a strange platoon. These good friends would look after me on these missions as only true friends would do. We never really got around to actually saying this to one another; it was simply there and we knew it.

Everything settled down to the evening routine of manning and securing our bunkers on the perimeter. All the claymores (hand-detonated anti-personnel mines) and trip flares were checked and reset. Company C lived on and controlled a steep hill designated as Hill 348 (348 being the number of feet above sea level). The top was ringed with bunkers and fighting holes, manned around the clock with the usual infantry weapons: M-16s, M-60 machine guns, grenades, M-79 grenade launchers, .50-caliber machine guns. We even had a "quad" .50-cal. (four synchronized machine guns designed as an anti-aircraft weapon), which we used against ground attacks. This awesome weapon was mounted on a heavy base on which it could pivot back and forth and up and down, covering the one side of the hill that had a gradual slope. This heavy machine gun, which could "blow away" light armor, could be used to clear "fire lanes" into the jungle. It would simply rip into the trees and undergrowth like a giant weed eater, cutting everything down for many yards. When all four of these guns were firing, the roar was beyond description, and I often shuddered to think what it had to have been like "down range" of this weapon. Of course, we had the usual several rings of concertina wire (coiled barbed wire) around the hill. That first evening, when I flew in on a supply chopper, I had gotten a good view of the shape of the hilltop and its defenses. There were several rotting bodies of the enemy hanging in the wire—they had been left as a warning!

The night became long. As usual, we took turns guarding our bunkers and manning the radio. There were "landlines" (telephone wire) running to each bunker, connecting each bunker with the command bunker. At predetermined time intervals after dark, we would call in a "sit rep" (a situation report). If nothing unusual had happened, the sit rep was negative. If anything had happened, like something or somebody probing our defenses, you called immediately; that call was to the command bunker, to our captain, the company commander. Most of these long nights were punctuated by our own H&I (harassment and interdiction) fire from our mortar team. This fire was random shelling of known trouble spots, trails, and suspected night movement areas of the VC, our enemy.

There's an art to training yourself to get rest when you're wet down to your socks and there are no bunks to lie on. You learn to curl up in a half-sitting, half-lying position, or you find a spot to stretch out and wrap yourself, from head to toe, in your poncho, keeping your head on the uphill side. Wrapping yourself like a mummy, including your head and face, had several purposes, one being that the nights in the monsoon season in the highlands were cold and naturally damp from constant rain. The poncho was wonderful for containing your body heat. Another reason we did this was to protect ourselves from the swarms of mosquitoes and the cat-sized rats that would move into our bunkers as soon as they were built. More than once, I've heard them scurrying on beams overhead in our bunkers and felt the dirt they shuffled off or felt them run across my still body. Since the face was the most vulnerable, being the main bare flesh exposed as we slept or tried to sleep in our damp boots and sweaty uniforms, we kept it covered. There had been some grunts who had been attacked by these aggressive rats, usually ending in chunks of flesh being ripped from their face, leaving a nasty wound and the ever-present risk of rabies.

Even though we had shifts, on and off, to guard our bunkers and man our radios, we always rested with our weapons and ammo right under our hands. The pitch blackness of the nights in the monsoon season were unforgettable, mainly because of the ever-present threat of instant death or of being severely wounded. The many things that became part of our survival instincts were complex "reflex-reaction" attitudes that allowed us some moments of rest when there was no threat. An example that comes to mind is learning to tell the difference between the sounds of incoming and outgoing mortar. Of course, it becomes obvious when an incoming mortar impacts. I'm referring to the sound a round makes as it leaves the "tube" or one passes overhead. In the infantry, you first learn to live with many sounds of modern weapons and what these sounds are telling you. Artillery rounds coming in, or passing overhead, sound like old train locomotives chugging along—though not as slow! The hollow sound a mortar makes as it leaves the tube can be picked up from a fair distance. The big worry is that after you've heard the sound, the mortar (depending on the range) has already been in the air for several seconds.

That particular night, in a heavy downpour of rain, our H&I mortar fire ended with a "short round," that is, the large "Four-Deuce" mortar (the size of a 105 mm artillery round) had one go off prematurely, approximately a hundred meters over our hill. (Sometimes very dense rain can detonate mortars or artillery shells by the mass of resistance to the nose cone in flight.) There was a tremendous explosion. I was on guard on top of the bunker, looking into the empty wet blackness, when the sky lit up like day and the concussion flattened my poncho down over me like a giant hand pushing me into the sandbags below. Where all the shrapnel went, God only knows—those were high explosives! For a long moment, I was seized by intense fear, thinking I was back in my wet darkness. Then I was overwhelmed by the realization of what had happened and that I had not been touched by the sting of hot, high-speed shrapnel! This was another night of close conversation with the Lord.

The rest of the night was uneventful but intense in the soul searching that was going on in my mind as I reviewed what could have happened to me, being completely exposed on top of that bunker. How very clearly I saw how quickly and easily I could have been cold and stiff, wrapped in my "old friend," my poncho, by the time the light of the sun again crept over the mountain range!

At a little after 0300, the Second Platoon was stirring and collecting their gear for the day's coming S&D. Their platoon leader stopped by my bunker and requested my presence in his group, which was assembling a little back and toward the center of the hill. As I was gathering and adjusting my gear, I noticed Monk and Chuck heading my way. Preparing to accompany the Second Platoon wasn't that big of a job, since whatever I hadn't worn all night I had within arm's reach. It was absolutely critical that you not have to search for these "tools" of survival when "hit" at night. Monk arrived first and was giving me encouragement with his easy manner and brotherly concern.

Monk and Chuck were point men. They were the ones who cut trails and led the rest of us through enemy booby-trapped jungle, who detected ambushes and got us from point A to point B through the use of a compass, good judgment, and instinct. Chuck came up then, carrying his flak jacket. He was acting a little strange as he edged me behind the soggy sandbag bunker; he obviously didn't want the rest of the men to hear what he had to say. As we snuck around to the back of the bunker, slipping in the mud, my eyes were fixed on his flak jacket. Chuck's jacket was an original. It had a number of colorful drawings and slogans, but the dominating part was the back, which had "California Kid" written on it in a fancy, colored scroll. His words were almost in a whisper, "Wear my flak jacket for luck, Doc." He was so sincere that I didn't even try to refuse.

The flak jacket we wore in Vietnam was heavy, somewhat cumbersome, and hotter than hell. It would protect you from many of the smaller pieces of shrapnel thrown off by grenade explosions and booby traps. It would in no way stop a modern needle-nose bullet; however, I have seen it save men from other high-velocity material. The thing weighed about sixteen to eighteen pounds and was terribly hot in the steamy jungle. The average grunt preferred not to wear one; in our company, however, the rule was "all medics wear a flak jacket on all missions." On my first mission, I learned the hard way that it demanded a price for its protection. That long day, I had foolishly left the hill with only two canteens of water and too much ammo! The jacket acted as a sauna shirt, sapping the liquid from my body. After that memorable day, I never left the hill with less than four canteens of water!

The conversation between Chuck and me centered around his concern for my safety. In his words, "Doc, those ******* will get you killed. If you get into some 'bad shit,' there's a New Testament in the right pocket and a rosary in the left." His straightforward, honest concern touched me deeply—more than he'll ever know. At this point, I had not known Chuck and Monk very long, and me being new at "humping the boonies," they had, by their kindness, helped me through very trying and worrisome times.

I clearly remember thinking that morning, as we moved single file down that dark, slippery trail into the musty jungle, how blessed I was to have found such good men who thought me worthy of their friendship. My next thought was, *Please, Lord, help me to be able to be worthy of their respect and friendship.* It's really strange what you think of when you live close to danger and death and are not distracted by a concern with material comforts. My most constant prayer was for His help when one of our men was wounded or dying. Of course, there was the ever-nagging fear of losing it and dying a coward among such brave young men. It wasn't that I didn't think I had it in me, but none of us really knew until we had been there. That day I would be tested again, and I feel that Chuck and Monk's concern and words were very important to my survival that morning. How does one express the warmth you feel in your heart just from a kind word or act that needs no explanation? Their words gave me much strength and would continue to do so later that day.

The morning was pretty much routine as we slowly crept down the slope into the wet darkness, with the point man (God bless them all!) feeling each step of the way with his trained boots and the tickle of hair on the back of his neck. We always left the hill under the cover of darkness so that the enemy would not know when and where we would be that day. The first rule of survival in the infantry in Vietnam was to patrol your A.O. (area of operation). If there was not constant contact and feedback on the

113

enemy, there was the danger of the enemy building up a large force around you and overrunning your position. In the Vietnam War, each group of infantry soldiers in the "bush" was an island, whose size depended on the type of operation you were involved in. A squad was from nine to thirteen men. A platoon had up to thirty-five men, and a company had up to 135 men. Your group had to protect themselves at all times on a 360-degree perimeter—there were no so-called front lines as there are in a conventional continental war.

After about forty-five minutes to an hour, we were down off the hill, out into the valley a fair distance and into the dense jungle by the time the first rays of sunlight turned everything into gray shadows. We took a short break at that time to collect ourselves and for the Lieutenant and point man to reaffirm our position, direction of travel, and next checkpoint (for mortar and artillery coordination). Already sweaty and tired from tension, I dropped down off to the side of the trail that the point man had hacked out for us with his machete. The place where we were resting was a stand of young bamboo trees—it was much like being in one of Dad's fields of tall stalked cane…but these kinds of thoughts had to be dropped quickly, for it was too dangerous to be daydreaming in the jungle. Mostly we blanked out our minds, a way to get more rest in five or ten minutes. I sat leaning into my gear and looking from face to face among the young men I was with. They didn't seem to be aware that I was tense and not that sure of myself. I was twenty-three; many of these boys hadn't even turned twenty yet, but they seemed to be handling everything as if they had been doing S&Ds for years. Each looked old and hard, each dealing with his own hell in his own way. It came down to each of us taking one day at a time and thanking God for that one…and not thinking about home. We shut down these conscious thoughts of home to the extent that "home" became just a vague dream back in our young life.

In the jungle, very little talking went on, and certainly not idle chatting; most commands and instructions were given with hand signals. The point man "talked" to us with body language. If he slowed, we slowed. If he pointed out a suspicious vine across the trail, each man in turn would step over it and stand waiting, pointing to the vine until the next man eased up to it and was aware of what was being pointed out. When the jungle thinned out, we lengthened the distance between the man in front and ourselves. When it became a wall of green and as dark as night, we were heel to toe. Those were the worst times. I remember almost panicking when I would lose sight of the back of the boot of the man in front of me. Oftentimes, he was a mere three feet ahead. When hit by the enemy in dense jungle, men full of adrenalin and tension can easily become disoriented and lost! I walked in the middle of the platoon, for protection and workability; however, I knew only too well that if I lost the man in front of me, I would split the platoon. When you add the idea of an ambush and the ever-present threat of tripping a booby trap that shred men and turned arms and legs into stumps, it's not hard to see why we did not fit in with our peers back home.

As I walked at a steady, even pace with those tough young American warriors, I was struck by the fact that not even one of them knew my name, nor I theirs, and yet our very lives depended on one another. Everything was like that. Vietnam was the "Real Disneyland," where the young took care of the young. Of course, my name was really not important, since all of us medics were called "Doc."

Having been honored with the job of caring for the soldiers and feeling great respect for them, I think we medics unconsciously tried to stay away from any close association with these men. Still, there were always some who touched your heart and scarred your soul when they were hit or killed in action. No matter how hard we tried to keep from a real friendship, there were always those whom you liked immediately, and they instantly got a "toehold" in your heart. I could not, or would not, have ever admitted this back in 1967 or '68, but now I can. My defenses are down, and my real emotions are starting to show signs of life.

We pushed on for hours through dense jungle full of thorned vines (wait-a-minute bushes) that hooked into every part of our uniform, gear, and flesh. I hadn't perfected the art of moving through tangled

115

underbrush, so I was getting slashed more than was necessary. In a short while, I had numerous bleeding scratches on my face and hands. My knees were catching it too, especially after I slipped off a rice dike, busting through my jungle fatigue pants. Later, when I looked myself over, I realized that I must have been a real sight, so much so as to be humorous to these tough grunts. I was slashed many times across the face, starting at the bridge of my nose and ending in horizontal scratches in line with my ears. The first impression I had of myself was that of a young Indian warrior with war paint on, mine being all red. My hands had some cuts, but the rest of my body had been pretty well protected by my gifted flak jacket, helmet, and uniform. (We wore our long sleeves down for protection from the jungle and its insects.)

About midmorning, we reached a small hamlet, which was another checkpoint. After scouting it and flanking it slowly until we were relatively certain it was safe to enter, we eased into the main area. What a wonderful blessing! There was a hand-dug open well with cool, clean water! Everything in this life that is essential for our survival, both physically and mentally, is magnified in the jungle. A man, especially a tough young man, in his prime, can go a long while without food, but the body cannot function long in an oven of heat and humidity without water. We cooled our bodies, both inside and out, with liberal amounts of that precious liquid. With our canteens full again and our brains refreshed, we moved out after carefully checking out the hamlet and finding no real evidence of the enemy.

The point man moved out, cutting out a trail through the back of the hamlet, stepping carefully and checking everything for booby traps and the many types of trip wires and trigger devices. The short stop and slowed pace in the hamlet, along with the cooling down with that wonderful well water, had given us a boost, but the jungle was very dense now, and each step demanded an extra effort, digging into our reserve strength. As I rounded a small hill, where the jungle thinned to let me see ahead, I saw the point man finishing a short climb and stepping into heavier foliage. For the next hour and a half, we pushed on through heavy, dark jungle. At times, there was hardly enough light to see where the man ahead was pushing through.

The tension grew to the point where I could taste it in my dry mouth. By this time, my flak jacket seemed heavier from sweat and was choking off the air that my lungs were screaming for. It was so hot and sticky with humidity that my very skin seemed to be grasping for oxygen. The bandoliers of ammo and the strap to my aid bag were cutting and riding over the collar of my flak jacket, slowing the surging blood trying to get through the arteries in my neck. So many things required me to be alert! I was desperately trying not to take my eyes off the man in front of me while pushing my tired body on, step after step, often bending low and pointing my helmet into the closing thorn bushes as the jungle boot ahead disappeared. As I pushed ahead, it seemed that not only were the vines and thorns holding onto every part of my gear and uniform, but they were pulling me back! Every now and then, my tired mind would send out a flash—"Be ready if they hit us in this mess!"—which caused a jolt of fear to flush the back of my neck with added heat. I thought I had known what ultimate weariness and utter exhaustion had meant from the days I had spent baling and stacking hay on hot summer days on the farm, back in the "world," a lifetime ago. Back then I had only begun to know what total exhaustion meant. In this dark green hell, we pushed our lean, tough bodies until we could only continue on sheer mental power—a tremendous strength, previously untapped in most of us. My biggest motivation was watching some of the toughest and bravest men of our country always pushing on around me. As one grunt put it, "We humped and humped until you couldn't take another step, and then we got up and went twice as far."

After an hour of this, which seemed to last forever, we took another short break. All of us collapsed back on our gear, right where we took our last step. Before letting my aching body shut down, I pushed handfuls of salt tabs to each man, reminding them to keep the water coming to their bodies. Most leaned into their helmets and chewed several tabs right then. My hip joints felt as though they were about to push through my lower back. I was tired beyond words, but at the same time lifted with pride just for being with men such as these. As I allowed my body to collapse back onto my gear, and after several salt tabs and a long drink from my canteen, my last vision of this strange dark world was of a number of half-inch-long black ants crawling over my chest. This brought absolutely no reaction whatsoever from my numb brain as everything became dark and wonderfully peaceful.

"Doc, Doc, time to move out." The ten-minute break had somehow lasted only a second or two. We were back on our feet readjusting all those chunks of weight hanging from our hips, back, neck, and hands. The RTO (radio telephone operator) was leaning forward again to keep the heavy pack-sized radio from pulling him over backward. The ever-moving flexible blade antenna telegraphed his every movement. The Lieutenant, who was always within an arm's reach of the RTO, signaled the point man to move out. The jungle had thinned out, and the rays of sunlight that showed through every now and then were welcome after that ominous darkness. After climbing and following the side of a hill, we came to a flat valley with a rice paddy. By the time I broke into the clearing, half the men were already a third of the way into the paddy, following the edge. About forty yards out in the flooded rice field, a farmer was standing stone-still behind his water buffalo and wooden plow. His head was bent down, his black silk pajamas hanging loosely on his thin frame. It seemed that every man clicked the safety off on his M-16 rifle, and the M-60 machine gunners shifted their barrels his way as they passed in line with him. As the whole platoon passed, the farmer never moved a muscle. As I looked back to see our last man, "tail-end Charlie," I saw him turn around and walk backward with his rifle leveled and sighted on the farmer's head. This was a "free fire zone," and anybody in the area was considered a possible enemy. Any male of military age (from early teens to old men) was a suspect. We had learned, all too often, that a farmer in his field could be hiding an AK-47 (a fully automatic Russian assault rifle with a thirty-round clip) and use it to cut down a group of our soldiers as they passed by.

After several more strips of foliage and small rice paddies, we started

118

across a rather large paddy. The point man and four or five of the first squad had gotten into cover on the other side when all hell broke loose! I didn't really hear those first rounds snap by us, but the explosion of automatic fire from the first squad ahead of me snapped us out of our trancelike drudgery with an instant surge of adrenaline. I turned to dive over a dike behind us. As I was diving, a strong black hand grabbed my web gear and helped me over with a powerful yank, causing me to literally make a flying dive to the back side of the two-and-a-half-foot dike.

Everything was chaotic. There were explosions of automatic rifles and machine gun fire on both sides of me. Men yelled to each other, and squad leaders gave commands for fire placement. I was inching my way back up the dike, sliding my M-16 rifle barrel over the crest when, again, I was pulled back hard from the rear. Before I could turn to see who pulled me back, I hear, "Doc, keep your damn head down! We're the target out in the open; the rest of the platoon will cover us!" The VC had opened up on us from a small hamlet about one hundred yards in front of our left flank, pinning the center of the platoon down. Both ends of our thirty-man platoon were under cover, returning fire. However, the rest of us were not able to see or fire back.

I slid back down to the base of the dry dike and could hardly believe the "coolness" of the M-60 gunner already sitting, leaning his back against the dirt bank. He had a cigarette hanging from his fingers as his machine gun rested across his lap. He said, "Doc, just take it easy. Don't be sticking your ****** head over the top. They'll tell us when they want us to move."

He seemed to be too relaxed, but then I was tense enough for both of us. I could tell immediately that he had been through this a number of times before. He was a big, strong-looking black grunt, with a controlled, serious look about him. As I think back on this scene now, decades later, I see the situation much more clearly than I did on that hot, sweaty, tense afternoon. He was doing more than taking a smoke break. He was watching our back side for any circling or flanking maneuver by the enemy. He also knew that you couldn't go very long out there all tied up in tense knots. You had to train yourself to react, but to do it with as little emotion as possible. Here in Vietnam, you came to a point where you really believed that if it was your time to go, it was your time to go and you couldn't do anything about it. Still, each of us had our own way of talking to God and preparing for our departure.

In the middle of these explosive noises, I hear the Lieutenant yelling for Seal (Walter Seals, the M-60 gunner who had pulled me back) to bring the machine gun up and for me to keep the rest of the men with us down behind the dike. What I saw next, I still find incredible. Seals casually flipped his cigarette out into the rice paddy and snapped on a full, 100-round belt of ammo and slammed the bolt back. He again reminded me not to stick my ****** head over the top. He gave me one more quick glance as he jumped to the top of the dike. The machine gun jumped in his arms as he fired from the hip, and dry dust kicked up behind his "lugged" jungle boots as he dashed forward, like a high school sprinter wearing spiked track shoes. He covered the forty yards very quickly, with grenades, canteens, and extra ammo belts flapping out from his gear. The whole scene was from a John Wayne movie, with enemy AK-47 rounds popping all around him. I almost expected to hear someone yell, "Cut! Great! Print!" The next thing I remember was a grunt, half-standing, half-crouching, with a LAW anti-tank rocket tube over his right shoulder aimed toward the hamlet. The blast of fire, heat, and smoke from the anti-tank rocket blew a cloud of dust up behind him as the rocket streaked across the rice paddy, trailing white smoke. There was a flash as it hit a thatched hut, and half a second later, the boom of the explosion rippled back to us. Before I knew what was happening, I found myself running with the rest of the platoon, charging the tree line toward the hamlet.

All around me there were M-16 rifles and several M-60 machine guns "barking." The M-60s were pointing out the targets to the rest of us with their long, red, deadly fingers. It really is amazing how revived and fresh the body can be when it is operating on massive doses of adrenalin! None of us had any problem sprinting the hundred yards to get at the VC. As we came upon the hamlet, the men on both flanks cut in from each side. The

VC had pulled their usual tactic of hitting us with everything they had and leaving before we could get to them.

The whole thing was over in about fifteen minutes. The men eased in and around several hooches. We searched out everything, but there was no one to be seen. There were cooking utensils on still-smoldering fires. Several wounded water buffalo were in makeshift pens, but no humans were to be found. While the grunts fanned out, treading very carefully, watching for booby traps, checking out everything, I stood with the Lieutenant and the RTO having a welcome smoke break. The men were very thorough; they checked out all the huts, haystacks, and surrounding jungle. A cave was found nearby, apparently used for storage. Several grenades were thrown in. As they exploded, dirt and dust belched out, taking my helmet with it. "Damn, Doc, I said, 'fire in the hole.'" It was a while before I stopped hearing all those bells. Luckily, the cave dropped down from the opening and the grenades went off below the opening, stopping the shrapnel.

Photo 19: Out on Patrol

Photo 20: Out on Patrol 2

Photo 21: Army helmet

Photo 22: Bomb crater

Photo 23: Sgt. Walter Seals

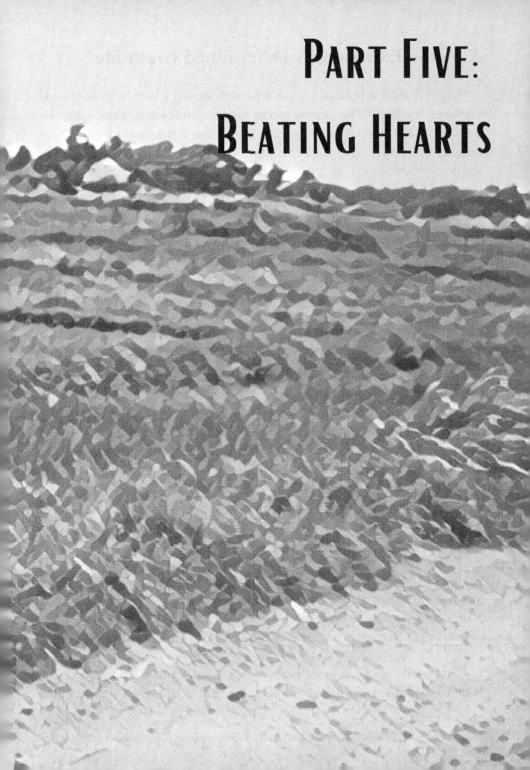

PART FIVE:
BEATING HEARTS

A Medic Experiences Determined Gratitude

The aid station bunker was alive with wounded grunts and wide-eyed displaced civilians. There were twenty-five to thirty-year elderly Mama-sans and young children squatting around the inside wall. One of our infantry units was engaged in a firefight with the Viet Cong near a village, and the villagers were in great danger, so the decision to evacuate them was made. Choppers were coming and going in quick succession, so we not only had the usual intense activity of caring for the wounded, we were getting all those poor, frightened mountain people (aka Montagnards) to understand we were trying to keep them safe.

The aid station was a beehive of activity with us medics and doctors doing what we were born to do. As usual, some cases were urgent, and the intense activity reached a fevered pitch.

After some long minutes of getting these cases stabilized and out to a Dustoff chopper to fly them to our surgical hospital in Chu Lai, we were able to relax our urgent care to a more normal level. It was at this time I was able to look around the bunker and notice those Mama-sans holding tightly to the small children and to see how concerned they were for what would be happening to them. I was struck by the fact that they had been put on our choppers and flown away not knowing where they would end up and if they would ever be back home again.

As I studied their faces, I had a chance to put myself in their world and imagine how badly they were in need of such a simple thing as drinking water! Having been taken from their home in the hot jungle and not even given a chance to bring water with them, I started handing out paper cups of our cool, fresh drinking water from our large metal cooler. They showed profound appreciation and gratitude. One of the most important elements of life, water—certainly in this part of the world—is highly regarded.

It was then that I noticed her: an old Mama-san was on her knees in front of me, kissing my dirty, bloody jungle boots. I tried to stop her, but she was not to be deterred. I have never been so humbled, or embarrassed, in all my days. I could not believe that something as simple as drinking water could be so highly valued for those poor souls!

F-4 Phantom Down!

I had finally gotten a couple of days off to go back to our base camp in Chu Lai to get a passport made for my R&R to Australia. After the usual red tape of paperwork and queueing up at several lines in different administration buildings, I had an afternoon free to roam on the beach and stop by an Enlisted Men's Club for some *cold* beer.

As I thoroughly enjoyed my long walk at the water's edge, I began collecting sea shells. I quickly noticed there was a wonderful variety of sizes and shapes. I thought of my youngest brother, Steve, who was still in grade school. I knew he would find them quite interesting and maybe take them to show-and-tell at school. We grew up on a farm in Kansas where life was busy with chores, field work, school. Our biggest adventure was traveling to the nearby state of Missouri for a long weekend camping trip. These shells from the other side of the world, about as far from Dad's farm as one could get, would be exciting for a twelve-year-old farm boy. Steve was much like me in that he was always looking for a new adventure and exploring the fields and pastures for interesting rocks and now and then a wonderful find—an arrowhead! We lived in the central plains of Kansas, where there had been many native Americans hunting and farming long before our ancestors came to the plains from Germany in the 1880s.

As I walked and smelled the South China Sea, felt the cool water healing my bare sore feet, I thought back to the days when I first arrived at Chu Lai. We lived in twenty-man tents near where I was walking and trained hard in our ten-day "charger" training to prepare for our one-year tour in the 196th Light Infantry Brigade. Near the beach, the Marine Corps had a runway where they flew F-4 Phantom jets out on air strikes. They were on twenty-four-hour call in support of the marine grunts as well as our army grunts. While we were training, we were constantly aware of these fighter jets. They screamed over our heads on takeoff and howled in with their flaps down as they landed. We were also aware of the ones that didn't come back. I had seen them in action later and learned to respect them greatly and to appreciate their bravery as they brought in bombs and napalm to save us, the infantry, in the jungle and rice paddies.

On this particular sunny, clear day, the Marine Corps F-4s were going out and coming back at a fairly constant rate. In fact, I remember making note of this and that all our combat infantry units, both marine and army, were involved in constant contact with the enemy. Today I could see that the F-4s were going out loaded with napalm canisters and bombs, which meant they were most likely supporting our grunts in the jungle. I also remember hearing our wonderful artillery batteries firing at constant levels, and by the number of guns firing at one time, I knew there were grunts out there in deep trouble.

Several times I stopped to watch our F-4s roar off the runway with both jet engines glowing red fire, their afterburners full bore. Since I was walking in an area on the beach that was at the far end of the runway, they were literally blasting over the top of my head; I could feel the heat from burning jet fuel. For some unknown reason, I was standing and watching one take off, his afterburners glowing. The jet was coming at me, and just as the F-4 was directly overhead, about 150 to 200 feet above me, there was a tremendous flash and explosion that rocked me back almost off my feet. Out of that ugly yellow fireball, debris was raining down all around me, and then the main landing gear with a tire attached bounced in the sand dunes about fifty yards in front of me.

In that split second, I witnessed two of our bravest of the brave (pilot and navigator) being vaporized and passing into eternity! Even though I had seen brave men die many times, I was totally stunned. There was no incoming fire, no problem that I had noticed, and yet their jet, with a full bomb load and a full fuel load, was gone in one giant explosion. It was another powerful example of how we all lived by the second, and death could reach us at any one moment, without even one second to prepare! These two highly skilled warriors were busy checking their gauges and final checklist, preparing for a dangerous air strike, when in a flash they were dead. The explosion I witnessed was so all-consuming, I truly doubt they found even a small part of these men to send home.

Photo 24: Location where the F-4 went down.

Please Save My Little Girl

As soon as Dr. Bob Klein got the call from over our bunker line, he and I headed down the hill with a medical kit to meet the young Vietnamese family. The situation was obviously critical as they carried a small child on a bamboo mat toward our aid bunker.

Within seconds, we were examining the beautiful little eight-year-old girl. This poor child was hit in the chest with a quarter-size razor-sharp piece of shrapnel, which had ripped a clean hole through her sternum. I can still see her tiny delicate heart struggling to keep going while we worked frantically to stabilize her. She needed a whole surgical team back at our surgical hospital in Chu Lai, thirty-five miles from our aid station. She had been in the wrong spot when a VC mortar exploded in her hamlet. The Viet Cong would often terrorize these poor people to make sure they weren't getting too friendly with us, the Americans. Dropping a few random mortars was just one of the ways! On my way out to our hilltop a few months earlier, I had experienced another very effective way to intimidate these people: I passed a dead Vietnamese man lying on the right side of the road, just a few inches near my feet as our jeep bounced along in the monsoon rain. Later I learned it was a typical VC terror tactic. This older man was the village chief, whom they had hung in the village square and later threw his body out on Highway One as a warning to all the local people. And so it went for these simple people, who wanted only to be left in peace to care for their families and live out their lives.

By the time we got a chopper inbound, this dear little child had gasped her last breath. It was hard for Dr. Klein as well as myself, but totally devastating for the young parents, especially the mother. She collapsed over her dead child, screaming and wailing out of control. This was very painful for us even though we had been toughened by many days of blood, suffering, and death. This tiny, beautiful child, innocent of the sins of war, put a wedge in our protective armor. I still see this young mother out of her mind with grief at the loss of her sweet baby girl.

As we served in Vietnam, we medical people had long since gotten past the shock of combat casualties, but when the death is totally wrong and pointless, as in the death of this child whose whole life was innocent play and love, left intense hurt and scars in the very deepest, private parts of our hearts. This child and parents have never been far from my often-recalled memories of this time in my life's journey.

Photo 25: We were constantly involved with the innocent children of the war.

Napalm

The ten-year-old Vietnamese boy was standing with his tiny frail arms held away from his body. Shreds of his clothing seemed to be hanging from his arms and legs... Oh God, no!!!... The awful smell of burnt flesh and the terrible screaming of some poor creature suffering unbearable pain shocked me to the reality of war. The boy had no clothes left on him. What I was seeing were strips of skin that had slipped off his body. Most of the skin on his legs had piled down on his ankles and around his feet. There was no hair left on this tiny frame, only small curled knots where it had melted and turned back on itself.

Never in my life have I seen or heard such agony!! May God forgive me, but the first thing I thought of was to put him out of this terrible hopeless hell of indescribable pain. Truly, the "raw" pain of burns to the flesh with all the surface nerve endings exposed to the 110-degree tropical air has to be one of the worst wounds to the mortal body.

This boy was caught on the fringe of a napalm attack on a village infested with the VC enemy. The enemy would often use innocent civilians as a shield to ambush our patrols, catching us in a horrific combat situation where civilians would suffer and be killed. These situations leave terrible guilt and many demons in our souls as we try to live out our years as normal people. Many of my brothers dread the nights when we need to rest our bodies and troubled souls, for when our conscious mind relaxes, the demons rule the subconscious.

I then noticed that his body was covered with fresh water buffalo manure. I cannot express my anxiety and rage at knowing this ignorant but well-meaning gesture had sealed his death sentence by covering him literally with billions of infectious bacteria. In a culture never exposed to modern medical procedures, nor the technology to inoculate people, the elders thought it would soothe the pain. In one instant, the flaming "jelly gas" clings to whatever it falls on, dying out only after it burns itself out.

We poured water slowly over his body as we gently dabbed away the manure with wads of gauze. The intensity of his pain increased as we rinsed away most of the manure and burnt skin. I could only hope that the cool clean water dampened some of the pain, if only for a few moments. Combat casualties are always to be reckoned with in war, but to witness painful, terrible deaths of the innocent children of war brings a life sentence of living with demons who will not let you forget.

After carefully wrapping this poor child in many layers of Vaseline gauze, we gently placed him on one of our Army Dustoff choppers and sent him to a Vietnamese hospital in Tam Ky. There, his own people would watch him die. Surely, man's war is Satan's finest accomplishment, for this boy's suffering and death created many more casualties on both sides of the earth with its lingering memories.

Number 25

We were taking a break, cooling down in the shade of a small village, where I had kicked back on my pack after checking on the men, making sure they had salt pills and water, when I noticed her. She was a feisty, little handful as she pointed out and did a sales pitch on her pots and pans hanging on all sides of her small shack. As I watched her, I was impressed with her persistent, indomitable spirit. Since I always had a special place in my heart for children, I was fascinated by the idea of a small child having to take on the burden of bringing in some income for her family.

As I walked up to her, she immediately turned on the sales pressure, sure that I was an easy mark. I was looking for a small pan to heat my C rations in, so as I examined different sizes and shapes of pots, she was giving me the usual rattle of "Hey, GI, you buy five dollars, five dollars?" In that part of the world, it was taken for granted that you bargain with anyone trying to sell or buy. So, I finally found a small pot that would serve the purpose and fit well in my ruck. As I started to haggle, she insisted on five dollars; I made ridiculous offers of fifty cents. We went back and forth until we got to about $2.50. When it seemed she was about to agree, I'd drop the price for the sole reason of seeing how much hassling she would take. It didn't take long until she was getting upset with my low bids and letting me have it with some four-letter words she obviously learned from some of my brothers.

After egging her on to the point of exasperation, she slammed the pot down with "you number ten GI!" In the simple language we would communicate in, number one was for very good and number ten for not good or very bad! When she said that, I knew I had her where I could really fire her up. I immediately said she was number twenty-five. With that she had a confused look, as she asked, "What twenty-five mean?" Taking great delight in carefully explaining "number one, way up here," my hand held above my head, "number ten down here," below my waist, "and number twenty-five way down here," close to the ground. That pushed her over the edge! With a whole string of four-letter words, all letting me know I was a no good **** GI, she started grabbing pots and pans off the rack and throwing them at me. I was laughing so hard I couldn't dodge all the pots that were flying at me; some were bouncing off my helmet, arms, and equipment. Since I hadn't laughed that hard in a very long time, it was the exact medicine I needed to lift my spirits. To say I loved every second of this explosion of pots and words would be an understatement. I immediately liked this kid!

After helping her gather up all her wares, as we were getting geared up to move out, I gave her five bucks (that is, five dollars in Military Payment Certificates (MPCs), the size of Monopoly money). I didn't care about the money; it was extra paper we had to carry and completely meaningless to me. One of my guys in my platoon asked, "Damn Doc, what did you do to her to get her that crazy?"

From that afternoon on, we became good friends as soon as she realized I did it just to fire her up. And every time we came into her village after that day, she would come running out to me as soon as she recognized me, with "Hey GI, hey GI," and I'd yell back, "Number 25." We'd talk the best we could with her limited English and my sign language, ending with a gift of whatever I had in C rations or a chocolate bar. Then, as all things in a war, one day it was the last time I saw her, without any way of knowing what became of her. She makes me smile even now, decades later, as I think of that dark-eyed, black-haired little pistol, always hoping she lived through that hell of a mess and found some happiness in life.

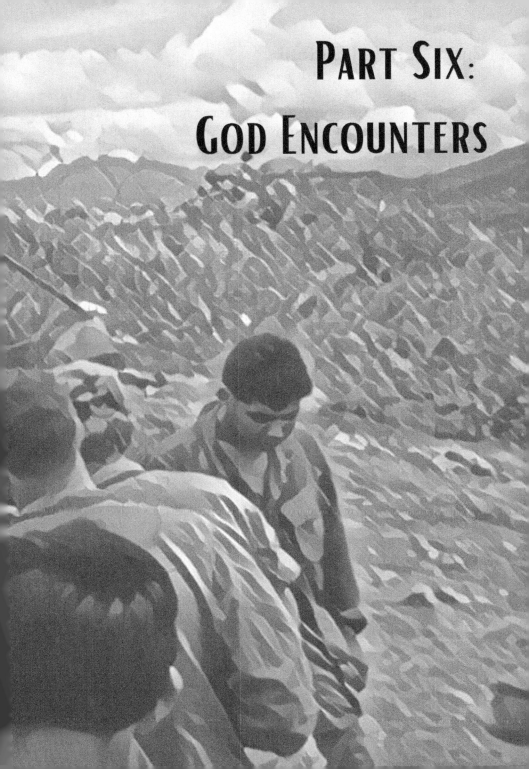

Part Six:
God Encounters

2nd Lt. Harold Clifford

From out of the pitch-black Asian night, the chopper hovers in…slipping sideways, causing the downpour of monsoon rain to become a swirl of fine mist curling back over the rotor. Even with the chopper's landing lights on, it's hard to see it clearly through the curtain of sadness.

The Dustoff chopper has more urgent casualties waiting for its return at the ambush site on Hill 63, so the pilot has the rotor trimmed out but the engine roaring with full RPM to lift off quickly…immediately after we unload its burden. We three medics are moving as fast as the slimy mud will allow with the litters we are carrying. There are several KIAs (Killed in Action), some walking wounded, and one young second lieutenant who is lying on a poncho that seems to be holding most of his blood. I can't reach him very well from the closest side of the open chopper, so I turn to run to the opposite side. What happens next seems like slow motion as suddenly I instinctively dig my lugged jungle boots into a stopping and reverse motion, realizing I'm slipping and sliding into certain death!!

The tail boom of the Huey chopper is rocking low to the mud as the Dustoff rests on the back edge of the skids. My boots were already under the blur of the almost invisible tail rotor and my face mere inches from this powerful man-size "meat grinder." I had, in a split second, made a terrible mistake.

It was standard procedure to always move around to the front of a running chopper. This was another time I owe my Divine Guardian my life!! All in one motion, my left hand grabs the muddy earth as I claw my body back the way I had come. Having only a second to compose myself, I run back around the nose of the chopper to get the lieutenant out and onto a litter. A thought strikes me like an electric jolt: nobody even noticed my near-fatal mistake. There is no time to dwell on that.

The lieutenant is cold and pale and appears to have already bled to death. The dead were being laid to the side as I carried one end of the lieutenant's litter. We're moving as fast as the slippery mud would allow, knowing that this man's chance of living, if there is a chance, is down to seconds. His is the most urgent case, so we lift him on a set of litter stands in the aid station bunker. Two of our doctors, Dr. Jamenez and Dr. Major "Mac" MacDonald immediately begin working on the .30-caliber bullet hole in the inside of his right thigh. The bullet had cleanly cut the femoral artery (the large main artery in the upper leg). Dr. Klein was doing "cutdowns" on both wrists and ankles. (This procedure calls for finding and cutting the main blood vessels in the extremities and inserting a small hollow tube to be connected to bags of whole blood.) I was on the right wrist, squeezing the bag injecting the blood as fast as possible. There was a medic on each of the other three cutdowns doing the same. As Dr. Jamenez and Dr. Mac struggle to find both ends of the femoral artery and to sew them together, the cold blood is pouring out the artery onto the litter to the point of running off the ends.

I then notice our beloved "Sky Pilot," Father Gariepy, leaning close to the lieutenant's right ear. The narrow ribbon of cloth, or stole, around his neck, used at the time of Last Rites, gently touches the dying lieutenant's shoulder. Father Bob Gariepy seemed to always appear, quietly and almost unnoticed, when that most critical moment arrived. Many of us in that blood-soaked combat aid station noticed, admired, and were deeply touched by his *total* commitment and loving concern for the salvation of the souls of these brave young American warriors. Each time I felt very honored and humbled while working near him. His presence seemed to calm and comfort souls, very noticeably, at those last minutes of life. I felt the strength of his presence around me whenever he appeared, even though he was humble and soft-spoken.

I'm watching him very closely now, as I put great pressure with both hands on the plastic bag, injecting "life" into the dying man. Father Bob is bent over, praying in the lieutenant's ear, "...oh, my God, I am heartily sorrowful for having offended Thee, and I detest all my sins because I dread the loss of Heaven and the pains of hell, but most of all because I have offended Thee, my God, who is all good and deserving of all my love."

Before my eyes, I see and hear an amazing thing happen. The lieutenant is still very cold and pale, but his lips are moving and repeating every word Father speaks into his right ear. By the end of the Act of Contrition—"I firmly resolve to amend my life"—the dying soldier's words are distinctly audible now, as his eyes pop open, roll back, and he gasps, "Where the hell am I?" At this point, our surgeons have connected the artery and the lieutenant has come back to life!!! I immediately recognize him as I look closely at his face. He was in my platoon for ten weeks at Fort Sam Houston, Texas, where we trained to be combat medics a year and a half earlier. He had just arrived in the 196th Light Infantry a few weeks earlier after being commissioned a second lieutenant.

As we rush him out to another waiting chopper to take him and several other critically wounded to our surgical hospital in Chu Lai, I yell in his face, "Clifford, Clifford, you remember me? We were together in Corpsman School at Fort Sam." I'll never forget that faraway, confused look as he looks into my eyes saying, "No, no, I don't remember you." I immediately feel foolish for questioning him at this most confusing and critical moment.

He disappeared into that dark, rainy, monsoon night, leaving me wondering all these many years if he really made it. But then, that is the way it always is at a forward aid station. There is no time for follow-up information on warrior brothers. There are too many waiting behind you, bleeding, dying, and suffering. I sure hope you made it, Lieutenant, and if you should chance to read this, it would make a part of my soul complete to hear from you and to know you made it.

(He died on the way to Chu Lai, that same night.)

Trust But Verify

It was another hot, dangerous day. Incoming mortars pounded Camp Evans. We had moved up north to operate in the A Shau Valley where the NVA were based. We, the 196th Light Infantry Brigade, were in joint operations with the 101ˢᵗ Airborne Division with whom we shared Camp Evans. This was in May of 1968, and contact with the NVA was regular and too often deadly. They obviously didn't appreciate two crack American infantry outfits in their home area, as demonstrated by the daily incoming 122 mm rockets and large mortars that rained down on Camp Evans.

This particular day, I was to catch a C-123 cargo plane heading back to Chu Lai, our base camp. Major MacDonald wanted me to check on and ready some medical supplies we needed to be flown up to us. We had a dirt runway where cargo planes supplied our infantry with ammo, grenades, machine gun barrels, C rations, etc. Naturally, the runway and cargo coming in regularly made us a prime target. Anytime you got near the runway, you had to be alert and ready to take cover. There was a walled-in protective holding area for aircraft readying to take off, for this was when they were most vulnerable from mortars or rockets.

A C-123 was warming up behind a sandbag wall where several of us army guys were waiting to catch a ride. A scout dog handler and I were waiting for the word on one going to Chu Lai. As this particular plane taxied around us, lining up with the runway, the airman in back was raising the back ramp. A sergeant with us yelled to us over the roar of the twin turboprop engines, "Hey, you two guys better get on that plane if you're going to Chu Lai!" Our C-123 ride was starting to move as we ran to the ramp and jumped onto it as the airman waved us to hurry. The pilot was revving the engines as he held the brake ready to give it all he had to get up and out as fast as possible when I yelled to the guy in back raising the ramp, "Are you going to Chu Lai?" He shook his head and told me they're going to Phu Bai. Grabbing the dog handler's arm, I yelled, "We got to get off, they're going to Phu Bai." Barely clearing the ramp as we jumped off the plane, we ran back to the protective wall as the pilot released his brakes

145

and hit full throttle.

Even as the full-throttled engines raised a cloud of dust in our direction, I could still see mortars hitting the runway ahead of him. Of course at this point, the pilot had no option but to fly through the exploding rounds. We all held our breath as the NVA walked the mortars down the runway toward the speeding cargo plane. With luck on his side, the pilot made it to the end of the runway and pulled up hard, immediately banking sharply to the left, turning away from the direction of the falling mortars.

Within seconds after he laid the left wing down to bank over the jungle, a stream of black smoke began pouring out of the motor on that side. With the loss of power at that critical moment, he started to lose altitude but leveled off with the nose up and did a belly landing in the muddy rice paddy. The water and mud of the paddy shot up and away from the body of the fuselage, and the plane quickly skidded to a stop. As the smoke swirled around the aircraft, I heard several of our helicopter gunships cranking up. Within a minute or two, they were over the crippled cargo plane, guns and rockets armed and ready with the door gunners leaning out, locked and loaded. They reminded me of hornets, angry and ready to attack. Any enemy crazy enough to try to take the crippled plane would have been dead before they got halfway across the rice paddy!

I later found out the left engine and wing had been shot up by small arms fire. As the pilot flew over the edge of the jungle, a light machine gun opened up on him. We had enemy all around us the whole time we were at Camp Evans, and they were always well concealed and quick to fire on us for any cause. They watched Camp Evans for any troop movements, resupply planes, gunships, choppers, or just any suspect activities.

Later that day, the scout dog handler and I caught a ride on another cargo plane heading back to Chu Lai with no real problems, just a few random mortars in our direction as we lifted off.

Photo 26: 2nd Lt. Harold Clifford

Lord, make me an instrument of Your peace.
Where there is hatred, let me sow love; where there is injury, pardon; where there
is doubt, faith; where there is despair, hope; where there is darkness, light; and where
there is sadness, joy.
O, Divine Master, grant that I may not so much seek to be consoled as to console;
to be understood as to understand; to be loved as to love; for it is in giving that we
receive; it is in pardoning that we are pardoned; and it is in dying that we are born to
eternal life.
Prayer of St. Francis

Thanks, Francisco

Francisco was the name I gave my Divine Guardian, my guardian angel. This story is of my actual face-to-face meeting with this guardian angel in a hellish black pit of lost souls in Tokyo, Japan. It all began on Hill 63, a camp in I Corps Vietnam, the northernmost of the four Corps tactical zones, the tactical zone nearest to North Vietnam and adjacent to the DMZ. Right after the Tet Offensive of 1968, I got a message from my first sergeant back in Chu Lai, our base camp, that I had gotten a five-day pass to Tokyo for some R&R (rest and relaxation).

I was to catch an Air Force C-130 turboprop cargo plane out of Da Nang on the northern coast of South Vietnam. This was the time just after my outfit, the 196th Light Infantry Brigade, in the northernmost part of South Vietnam, had been in some brutal, bloody combat with the NVA, a time when our brave troopers, the grunts, were in contact with the enemy pretty much day and night. I was really looking forward to some sightseeing in a nonlethal environment. After all the killing, dying, and stacking my brothers on piles to begin their journey home, I was in desperate need of a break. However, if I'd known what awaited me in Tokyo, I'd have stayed with my brothers and continued my duties as a medic.

The whole adventure began with ominous feelings of impending doom. Eight of us army guys boarded the C-130 and strapped into web seats on the outer edges of large, chained-down pallets of freight. The weather was bad!

It was 10:30 p.m., and we were headed dead into a typhoon over the South China Sea, facing horizontal rain and ten hours of flying time. *Praying for calm wisdom and acceptance of my trials had become automatic, so I put a few more miles on the rosary Father Gariepy (our Catholic chaplin) had given me.*

That wonderful, tough plane and brave pilot held on hour after hour of turbulence, rising a couple hundred feet one instant and next lurching three hundred feet down. The pilot told us that there were forty-foot swells on the ocean and that if we went down with the plane to get those damn jungle boots off and stay with the plane because it will float for a while…but I was too busy praying to ask how long "a while" was. And if that wasn't enough stress, every now and then, a lightning bolt the size of a man's arm would crash into and splash across the length of the wings. Since I was next to a window, the strike was brilliant even with my eyes closed in deep communication with my only True Friend.

I don't remember a lot during this silent pleading for survival until about the ninth hour when we finally broke through the darkness just as the sun was coming up. The moment we broke through the storm clouds, the sun was peeking over the vast Pacific Ocean. What a wonderous sign of hope to see this great ocean's other face—calm, smooth, and at peace! The water was flat and calm, with bright, warm sunlight reaching out to us from the end of the earth. I was suddenly in the presence of my Divine Creator! Little did I know this was only the introduction to an implausible adventure I'll always remember as a time I was thankfully sent divine help. The past forty-plus years have not dulled even the slightest memory of this unnerving experience.

After landing at Tachikawa, our U.S. Air Force base in Japan, I was simply content with the strange new world and being thankful for the time away from the battlefield. After joining up with two of the army grunts I had flown in with, we agreed on a nearby hotel and checked in. Wandering the big city of Tokyo was very interesting and rather awesome. I thought of our fathers' generation who fought in World War II to stop this country from totally annihilating our country and taking away our hard-earned freedoms.

That first morning as we came out the front door of the hotel to begin our adventure, I saw the kindest, most gentle soul in the form of an elderly Japanese lady. She stood behind a small pushcart loaded with delicious sweet rolls. Even now, I can still see her kindly face and low bow as she greeted us with "O hi O," (spelled *Ohayo* in Japanese, a casual morning greeting). She literally brought sunshine to my morning, warming my soul as I began my day in her world. Each morning I was greeted this way, and as I paid her for my sweet roll, she would teach me a new Japanese word or phrase. Certainly some souls are placed in our paths in life to change or encourage us; she gave me hope for humanity.

We wandered down the *Ginza* checking the many stores, vendors, and coffee shops and tried many different Japanese foods; some went down better with their very smooth rice beer. Somewhere in all this investigation of new foods, I made friends with two local Japanese students who had been studying the English language and were anxious to try out their new skill on me. One of these young men had a girlfriend who seemed quite content to tag along as they enthusiastically introduced me to their culture. We visited Buddhist temples and beautiful watery flower gardens and hiked to the top of Mt. Fuji. Mt. Fuji is an impressive snow-capped volcanic mountain with many old pagodas and Buddhist shrines along the trail to its summit.

My new friends even took me to, and up to the top of, the Tokyo Tower (a twin to the Eiffel Tower in Paris). What a view you get of this vast city! I couldn't help being overwhelmed by sadness knowing how different this view was a mere twenty-three years earlier when our air force firebombed this city.

As we wandered through the streets of this great city, I sensed and sometimes saw resentment of us Americans in the faces of some of the older people. (In retrospect, we returning Vietnam veterans would also feel resentment from our fellow U.S. citizens for our part in a war!) But then I thought of that dear little old lady in front of our hotel, and I felt hope for us all! I can still see her smiling face, which began with her eyes. I never felt a lack of love radiating from her whole being. She is surely one soul I'll most likely meet in heaven!

All was well until the third day when I decided to hang out with the two grunts who were staying at my hotel. This would lead to an adventure into an unsettling dark world never experienced by me before. I hesitate to use the term "ugly American," but it seems to come to mind whenever I recall this experience.

These two young men I was with were good soldiers—perhaps too good. By that I mean, combat is a terrible, soul-warping world where one must steal oneself from normal feelings and compassion for life in order to survive. The first clue I got that I should have distanced myself from them was a half-drunken remark to some nearby Japanese men working on a street project. One of the soldiers shouted something to the effect of, "Remember Hiroshima, you *******!" The word Hiroshima was understood, and I saw the immediate hatred it brought out of these local men. This was a lesson I made a central part of my decision-making from that day on: be very in tune with my first intuition.

I'm still not sure as to why I allowed myself to continue with them, when everything in me said not to. I had a number of afternoon hours to make my move but did not. When that taxi let us off in the deepest, darkest hole that evening, where train cars, sooty rails, no streetlights, and dirty dark warehouses were all around, I knew I was sinking in over my head! I still get chills when I think of my journey down underground through that four-foot-high tunnel with three checkpoints of doors and armed guards. These guards were tough-looking muscular young men with tattoos, wearing muscle shirts and carrying a straight razor in their back pocket, which they reached back to cover with their hand as we passed through.

All along the length of the tunnel (sixty to seventy feet), there were three-foot by six-foot pockets cut into the walls, dimly lit by tiny colorful bulbs and screened by a curtain of hanging beads. Behind the beads, one could discern couples staring back with the blank eyes of someone in a drugged stupor.

After about seventy-five feet, this tunnel opened into a dark underground room approximately forty by sixty feet packed with young Japanese men and women dancing and lounging on small cushions around low tables. I'd never been in a so-called "opium den," but I'm sure this was the human "hell" I found myself in. I tried to make myself invisible and prayed with all my being that I was. A man next to me on one of the floor cushions had a volleyball-sized plastic bag with a fine white powder in the bottom which he blew up, slapped the bottom, turning the powder into a white fog, and inhaled. The fellow immediately rolled over on his back, his eyes rolling back, appearing as if struck dead! I don't remember most after this, but I prayed from the deepest part of my soul to be somehow delivered from this Dante's Hell! The two other American soldiers and I were the only Caucasians in this room of over thirty couples. We were very much noticed and not welcome. Just when I felt I was in the pit of despair, it got worse!

One of my drunken companions decided he wanted to dance with one of the young Japanese girls who already had a partner. He boldly strutted up to the couple, rudely pushing her male partner out of the way as he grabbed the girl. This was the point when I decided if I had even a chance to get out alive, I should make my move immediately!

I have never felt as hopelessly alone and in imminent danger of death as I made my way to the first door. I had seen death all around me, experienced bleak hopelessness, and walked through the valley of death in 'Nam, and yet, I had never felt so alone! In 'Nam, there were always "brothers" to die with; here I was not only 10,000 miles from home, but I was lost in a place where no one understood my words and wouldn't give a damn if I was alive or dead.

I made my way out the same way we had entered, down that dark, dank tunnel, confronting each guard in front of the small door, with hands shoulder high, palms out slowly, pointing ahead in a way that hopefully they'd see my sincere desire to simply be gone. Each hesitated, showing pure hate in his manner as one hand gripped the handle of the straight razor in his back pocket. Slowly, very slowly, each stepped aside, tense as a predator ready to spring. The third and last man held his ground and slowly drew his razor out of his pocket and flipped it open in my face.

A great calm came over me, a calmness that only happened when, in a desperate situation, I felt the breath of death in my face. At these times, I felt a real presence of my Divine Savior.

After several long seconds of slowly shaking my head and again pointing out in a calm, peaceful manner, he ever so slowly stepped aside, watching my every move, tensed to kill.

After clearing the last few feet of the tunnel, it simply dumped me back out into the black abyss of no people, no idea where I was, and no hope of finding my way out! I encountered those same dirty, dark train cars; no light except for the glow of the city shone over those dingy, dirty warehouses. I made my way to a dirt trail that seemed to run through this hell. Not knowing what to do or which way to go, I stood stone still and prayed for a miracle.

In a few minutes, I saw headlights coming my way. Within seconds, I realized it was a cab. Without hesitation, I stepped into his path and waved for him to stop. In that instant, he swerved and accelerated away! I knew then I was doomed, for as soon as he saw I was Caucasian, he wanted no part of me.

I have read that your prayers are at their absolute "purest" when you're hanging by a thread, and even that thread was unraveling for me.... It was then that I saw him. I don't remember anything about how he got there, just him simply standing across from me on the other side of the trail, ten feet away. He was literally glowing in an all-white suit, decked out with two professional-looking cameras across his chest and, of all things, a white Panama hat! He was a middle-aged white male who asked in an Australian accent if I was an American. And when I answered that I was, he replied, "Stay where you are, I'll come to you!" He spoke with calm authority and a compassion that gave me instant peace. He stepped across the trail to me, standing a mere three feet from my stunned face. After a long moment of staring into his eyes, he said with great concern, "You're in a very bad place, and you need to get out of here now!" I think I mumbled something like, "You're telling me, brother." He responded with, "Wait right here," as he leaned into the darkness waving his hand. Immediately there were headlights coming our way, just as before, only this time, the cab stopped. He reached behind me, opened the back door, and told the driver something in Japanese. He wrote something in Japanese characters on the inside of a matchbook, handed it to me, and told me to hang onto it and don't lose it. He then informed me he had told the cab driver to take me to a hotel where they are all Japanese but that they speak perfect English. I should tell them the name of my hotel, and they, in turn, will instruct the driver to take me there.

As that stale, tobacco-reeking cab shot me out of that hellhole, I sank into the back seat with relief and elation that can only be experienced when you have clearly seen the face of death and have been spared. I was so caught in the moment of salvation that I never thought to glance back, but I have no doubt that he was gone as quickly as he had come.

The rest of the story is anticlimactic and went exactly as the man in white had instructed. This all was much like being in mortal combat; your whole being is so busy in the survival mode that there is no moment for logic or emotions.

Only after I was safely sitting on the edge of my hotel bed did it sink deeply into my being as to what had actually taken place. The timing, the miraculous appearance of a man in a snow-white suit with expensive cameras, making him a ridiculously easy target to be robbed, was astounding. His absolute sole purpose, to save me, caused deep reflection and soul searching as to what my true purpose was in this life! Most of that night was spent lying in that dark safe room staring at a blank ceiling feeling very blessed and wondering if it had all been a dream.

Even though I had two more days of leave left, I was packed and off to the air base early the next morning. I'm sorry to say, I never saw my dear little friend out front that morning and have often prayed she had a good life. As I walked away from that strange world, I couldn't help smiling in my mind, wondering if that sweet little Japanese lady wasn't a good friend of the man in white.

The two days I spent waiting for a flight back to my outfit were uneventful, which was okay with me. I slept on a wooden bench in the air terminal eating out of a vending machine. Words fall short describing the strange peace and contentment that had settled into my view of life. I felt calm and willing to accept whatever might be waiting for me in that strange land of untold sadness called Vietnam.

Saying Goodbye to Charlie Company

It was the end of September 1968 and my tour in 'Nam and my time in the army were up. My platoon was saddling up for another search and destroy mission. It was a dark rainy morning on Hill 348. The men were busy preparing their gear for a long day of pushing through dense jungle and steamy hot open rice paddies. We always moved off the hill under the cover of early morning darkness, blending quietly into the timeless unknown. Each day out there would be a memory of lost youth, accelerated aging and the beginnings of a potential recurring nightmare.

As we prepared to move out, my Platoon Leader, Lt. Harris, came up to me and told me to stay back on the Hill and take the resupply chopper back to Hill 63 LZ Baldy. I clearly remember his heartfelt statement, "Doc, go home, you're not missing anything here." There is no way I can relate the mixed emotions I felt. I was not filled with relief or joy, only a sense of loss of letting my brothers down, of simply taking care of my own safe world and leaving them in their "world of hurt."

I stood off to one side as they filed by, each man in turn giving me a precious-to-me gift. Some of the gifts were their "lucky last beer," rubbed shiny from many tense hours stowed in their ruck, their backpack. Another's gift could be a lucky soda that survived a bad day. Each had a few words of friendship or a request to remember them when I was back in "the world." Things like "Doc, say hi to one of those sweet little babes when you're dragging main street." Or simply, "Doc, say hi to the world for me." This was the first time in my long year that I had tears running down my face—I was thankful it was raining.

Photo 27: Last Day in Vietnam

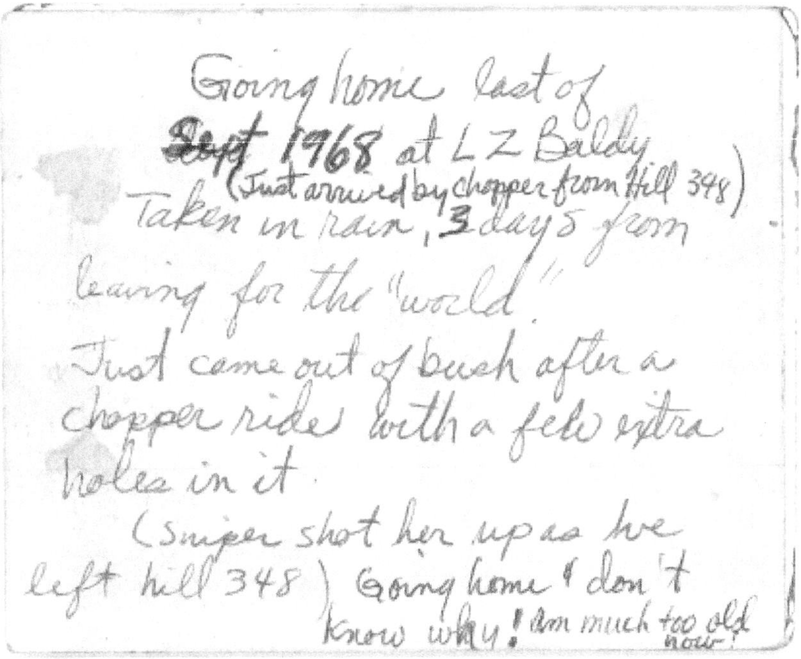

Going home last of
~~Sept~~ 1968 at LZ Baldy
(Just arrived by chopper from Hill 348)
Taken in rain, 3 days from
leaving for the "world."
Just came out of bush after a
chopper ride with a few extra
holes in it
(Sniper shot her up as we
left hill 348) Going home & don't
know why! I am much too old
now!

Photo 28: Writing on the back of Photo 23

Welcome Home?

After a long, quiet flight with one short stop at Clark Air Base in the Philippines, we touched down in the "world." In a few short minutes, we were standing in shock on the concrete runway in Seattle, Washington. Our time in the unfriendly, steamy, oftentimes lethal jungles of Vietnam seemed unbearable and unending, and now, suddenly, those days of extreme physical and mental fatigue had miraculously ended.

The Washington state sky was overcast, and the air had a chill to it as we each were flooded with deep feelings of pride for having served our country faithfully. Some of us knelt to kiss our homeland's soil. No one can really appreciate what this country means until you have been outside of her, lived and fought for every freedom that is taken for granted here. One must live the "price" and see the amount of heroism and blood those "Stars and Stripes" represent.

But some soldiers' time in service would not end. On troop arrivals, the army did not allow family members to greet their returning soldiers out on the tarmac. But one mom managed to bypass that rule and ran out to meet her son. The son reacted badly; he thought his own mom was Viet Cong and was trying to ambush him. He did not recognize her in any way. What a price that mom paid then and would continue to pay throughout her life. "You're never finished" was the mantra of many Vietnam veterans.

Of course, we now know our safe return was not proudly hailed by all. I shall never forget the angry, stunned, and lost feeling I had as I stepped off my "Freedom Bird" in the Seattle airport. As we filed off to the air terminal, our welcome home banners read, "We don't want the baby killers here," and "How many women and children did you murder?"

Some of us had fellow Americans spit in our faces as they asked those same dishonorable questions. If those protesters' intentions were to wound and hurt us, they should know they were more effective than the

NVA we had been fighting in 'Nam. In all of the history of this powerful, great country, there has never been such a degrading, dishonorable "slap" to our returning warriors, to men who fought bravely and with honor, enduring extreme hardship and pain in a foreign land, the same as all our brothers in wars before us. None of us were prepared for this "mantle of shame" our countrymen placed on our shoulders. How, then, were we supposed to go back to a homeland that did not care about our friends who had died in our arms, who did not want to know of our aching hearts and torn souls? Many of my brothers are still not healed from this festering wound. It's still very hard for me to understand why these same men were treated more like criminals, losers, the dregs of our society rather than the brave patriots they were.

After passing through customs, I and two other "brand new" buck sergeants pushed on into the airport lounge to toast each other on our safe return. We toasted to our lost friends and toasted the fact of us just being alive! The lounge was empty but for one graying businessman, sitting off in a corner. As we allowed ourselves to let down, just a little, and to openly congratulate each other with handshakes and pats on the shoulder, we noticed the middle-aged man beside us. He was well dressed, the executive type, with a neatly trimmed haircut with just a flare of gray on each temple. He had come up to pay for his drink and to tell the bartender, "Give these boys anything they want, and all they can drink, and put it on my tab." We all three stood to thank him and to introduce ourselves, when again, good intentions were returned with a sad look as he slowly shook his head and left. Was he disapproving of the fact that we were willing to volunteer our lives to fight for a country and people on the other side of the world, or was he disgusted and ashamed that our political leaders had sent many young Americans into a conflict that exposed a whole generation to the horrors of war? We would never know.

After one more round on the stranger's tab, we were off to catch a bus to Fort Lewis to process in and, for me, process out of the army. My two years with the U.S. Army were up, and it was time to get on with life "in the world." We were funneled into the usual long lines that are simply

160

accepted after several years in the military. There were more forms to be filled out, ones for final pay vouchers, for clothing and equipment owed the Army or to be turned in. Instead of a discharge physical to verify any wounds or injuries, we were told not to worry about it but to keep the line moving. In one of the final lines, we were measured for a new Class A uniform to go home in. This they did a pretty good job of; they had my Americal Division and Unit 196th Light Infantry Brigade unit patches sewn on right, with my new sergeant stripes on each sleeve, with overseas bars and combat stripes. We were issued everything—shoes, socks, shirt, tie, hat, brass, and a belt— so we could wear the uniform home and hang it in a closet for our future children to wonder about. Some didn't even wear their uniform home. We were advised it might be wise to go home in civilian clothes. Not for me. I am proud of the men I served with and the unit we were in and of those heroes who paid my way home. Many of us felt that pride and dared anyone to challenge us.

The flight back to Wichita, to the same airport I had left a lifetime ago, was rather uneventful. A few passengers stared at my uniform, more out of curiosity than interest. Our army uniform looked noticeably different than the way it did before we left. We wore several rows of ribbons (which represent medals earned) along with either a CIB (Combat Infantry Badge) or, for us medics, a CMB (Combat Medical Badge). The combat and overseas marks we wore on our sleeves gave us away, punctuated by a nervous, detached look that we were not even aware of. In retrospect, I see clearly how we did not blend in with the relaxed, self-oriented, unaware people around us. As we traveled through the airport, the plane, and once again our home terminal, we had automatically been aware of every sound, every movement, and even the attitude of people in our "safety zone." This super awareness is a product of honing the kind of survival instincts that are learned in the jungle but usually not necessary at home.

It was about 9:30 in the evening when the plane dropped down into the sea of lights that the captain said was Wichita, Kansas. The hustle and excitement of the last two days had lulled me into a dazed state. I felt no elation, nor joy, as we had all dreamed it would be so many times, the way we just knew it would be. I carried my small AWOL bag off and headed to the baggage area to pick up my duffle bag. I dug out my duffle, and an old friend who worked with my older brother, John, at Braniff Airlines was there and insisted he would carry my bag. I had known Pat from days of house-building before I had gone into the army. In but a couple minutes, I was sitting on my bag staring out into the city lights, wondering what the hell I was doing home when there were men dying and wounded, waiting to be cared for back in the "real" world—a place where lifelong friends were preparing for another day, hoping and praying it wouldn't be their last.

After several rings, mom answered the phone. She sounded as if I were hearing her in a dream. She said that she and Dad would be there as soon as possible. The airport was dark and void of people when Dad and Mom came up to where I was sitting. I guess I was lost in a kaleidoscope of thought. Mom rushed up to me with open arms, and all I was able to do was stand, cold and confused with my arms limp, unable to return her embrace. How would I ever be able to explain to her that this was all that was left in me?

Photo 29: Trying to fit in again, back in "The World"

Brothers

I was home about a week when I found myself in a local town intending to buy and send a six-pack of beer to Joe and Charlie. I had promised them that I would prove that we had Coors Beer in Kansas, since these Californian boys were sure it was all sent to them. I had a hard time convincing them that Coors was made in our next-door state, Colorado. Many times they had told me how great it would be to have a Coors beer from the world!

So, when it got close to my time to go home, I promised them I would send them some as soon as I got back to the world. I carefully wrapped each of the six cans of Coors in newspaper and packed them tight together, so they would not be damaged on their long trip to 'Nam.

It was about 22 years later when Joe and Charlie finished the story for me. They said they were blown away that Doc was the only one that had come through on a promise made to remember them when he got back to the world. They told me the first two Coors were selfishly guzzled down by them, and the other four were saved for a "stand down" back at base camp, when our company would get to rest for a few days.

The story ended with those four cans of Coors beer carefully poured into 52 small pill cups at a special gathering of 52 of my brothers, where "Charlie Tigers" toasted to the world and to the "Doc" in Kansas who remembered them!

Postlude

After having lived a long life as a husband, father, and grandfather with many blessings, I'm still trying to adjust to this safe, self-centered world, a world where our fellow Americans are more interested in their own comfortable lives than to have any concern for our "world of hurt." It's beyond any of us to explain what happened to us after being a survivor of a world that the protected will never know! To quote a brother from his book, *My Story*, Gary Lyles tells of his time in Alpha Company, Third Battalion, 21st Infantry, 196th Light Infantry Brigade in 1968, "not in a billion years would my family or friends ever imagine what I saw, what I did, what I had to live through!"

I have never been so honored, so humbled, no more certain of my job than when I was assigned to the 196th Light Infantry Brigade as a combat medic in 1967 in I Corps, four months before the Tet Offensive of 1968. The absolute crowning moment was when I stepped off the resupply chopper on Hill 348 (LZ Center) and became a "Doc" for Charlie Company, First Platoon, Third Battalion, 21st Infantry, the "Charlie Tigers."

In all the many years since I came home from Vietnam in September of 1968, I have been driven to tell my story in a way that would represent all my brother combat medics and Navy corpsmen who will never be able to tell their story. those who died so valiantly and unselfishly for their fellow soldiers, and for those who will not or cannot ever speak of those terrible days.

I sincerely hope that you, the reader, can feel and understand how we not only had great respect for these men, but a grave responsibility to always be there for them. They had become our family! This left us open to carry a lifetime of hurt, regret, and soul-searching pain from when it wasn't humanly possible to save their precious young lives, which in turn connected us forever to their "gold star" families. I have always felt greatly honored to have been able to be there for them and to offer my life to save them. Having been tied so closely to their lives, I know I'll be there for these combat "grunts" until my very last breath.

Photo 30: (From left) Joe "Monk" Mendoza, Sgt. Dave "Doc" Hilger and Lt. Col. Chuck Horner, 23 years after the war.

Acknowledgments

As with any complex project it takes a number of people who care and believe in it to get it done. I owe a big part of my healing and being able to talk and write about Vietnam to my cousin, Deanna Gouch and her husband Dale. Deanna was a high school teacher who invited me to talk about the war in Vietnam to her seniors; I did that for almost two decades. These young people showed the respect and interest as to what happened to us; that made us feel welcome and respected.

I thank my oldest granddaughter, Raeley, who took it on her own to put my stories on the computer. She was very encouraging and inspired me by telling me that this would be my legacy to my grandchildren. Love you, Raeley!

The one person I owe the most to would be Richard Gariepy, my friend and brother 'Nam vet who served in the Army as a Captain in an airborne unit.

He is a brother to my hero and dear friend, our "Sky Pilot," Father Bob Gariepy. He was the one person that really believed in the need to tell "our story." <u>But mostly he believed in me</u>! He put in a lot of hours getting stories to other veterans and publishers. I will always remember you, Richard, for getting me started and keeping me going down that long road. You being Father Bob's brother makes you part of my family.

To our parish secretary, Renee Seifert, who volunteered to type my complete manuscript and put it on the computer. She made me look pretty good, I didn't know I spelled that well! She did all this after working a day job and working it into her evenings after being a wife and mother to her family. Thanks, Renee!

A special thanks to Nika Sykes who, through a chance meeting, connected me with my publisher, Air Capital Press LLC. When she told me her grandpa (Ed Sykes, a famous jet fighter pilot who was a hero in the air war over North Vietnam, Cambodia and Laos and flew 118 missions in an F-105 Thunderchief) had written a book and also had a publishing company with his wife Mary Sykes, I could hardly believe it. I am very thankful to my editor, Mary Sykes and to my book designer Mandy, Mary and Ed's daughter, who put the final polish and shine on my humble work. Thank you Ed, Mary and Mandy!

Thank you, thank you—for allowing me to honor my many brothers after 54 years. How can any of us, that for whatever divine plan, were allowed to come home and thank those that gave everything so that we could have a life? So we could know the sweet unconditional love of a child sleeping so peacefully, so totally loved, snuggled close to your heart and feeling their gentle breath on your neck. I have been allowed to experience this with all four of my children, Ariana Daren, Larrisa and Devon and all of their children, my grand kids, all 21 of them: Raeley, Alaina, Grant, Sophia, Faith, Ayden, Conner, Joseph, Luke, Katelyn, John, Daniel, Ryan, Claire, Genevieve, Vivian, Arionna, Cora, Damon, Brynlee and Mia.

None of this would have been possible without my wife, Sherry, the one person who gave birth to my children, loved, protected, kept them healthy and made sure they were well educated and prepared for life's ongoing challenges. We, my wife and I, always made our Catholic faith and love of our Lord the center of our journey here on Earth. Mostly I thank my Lord Jesus for always being my best friend and most loving father! He is the reason I was allowed this life!

A big part of my life after Vietnam is the result of the friendship and resulting brotherhood that I was honored to experience with fellow wartime men. Joe Mendoza--my hero—a grunt that is ten feet tall to me. Charlie Horner—also my hero, a grunt and ten feet tall. Doctor Bob Klein, a very special human being with a pure loving heart responsible for saving many young troopers, not to mention children. He always had a special love for children. He is now retired after a long life loving and caring for children as a pediatric surgeon. He and I had been very close in Vietnam and all these many years after. What an honor to have Bob Klein, Joe Mendoza, Charlie Horner, Rich Mosher, Father Bob & Richard Gariepy, Dr. Scottie, Dr. Jamenez, Dr. MacDonald and Tony Adias, Larry Lane, Jay Goodrich in my life.

About the Author

My life is really not that special. I grew up on a typical small farm in Kansas. I went to grade school in a small town about three miles from the farm. From the time I was old enough to carry a bucketful of milk, I was helping with the farm work.

I went to a local small town high school and then on to college at Pittsburg State the fall of 1963. I was in Army ROTC for 2 ½ years, but decided I didn't want to be an officer and would rather be with "the grunts" sweating in the mud with the men that fought and were my heroes.

My final days are living and loving my children, grandchildren and still being a "Doc" to the survivors of the war that nobody gives a damn about. We always knew all we had was each other! I feel my life has done a full circle with my being a hospice volunteer for Harry Hynes for the past 15 years. This is the last part of my destiny after providing for and raising my beloved family and becoming who I am after living through my time in hell.

Picture Index

The following photographs are from my days in Vietnam. I am not a professional photographer, but I took a lot of pictures, and some were snapped almost without any forethought to what I was capturing. I just knew that I had to take a picture right then and there. Although there is not a caption on these photos, there is a story behind each one. But I know there will also be a different story than my own, that another veteran will be able to tell using the pictures that I snapped. I think, in my heart, I knew I was taking these pictures for all of us.

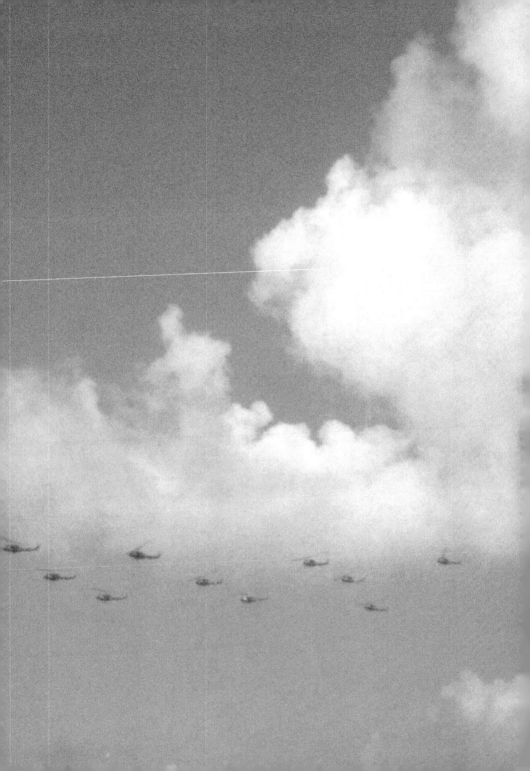

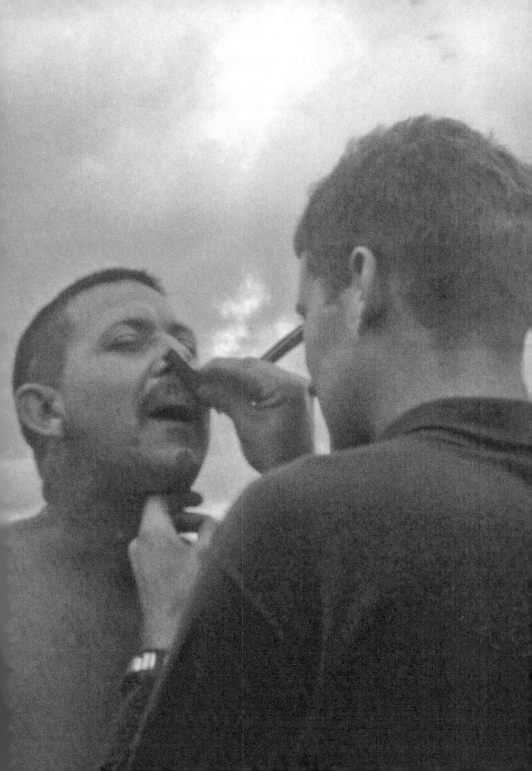

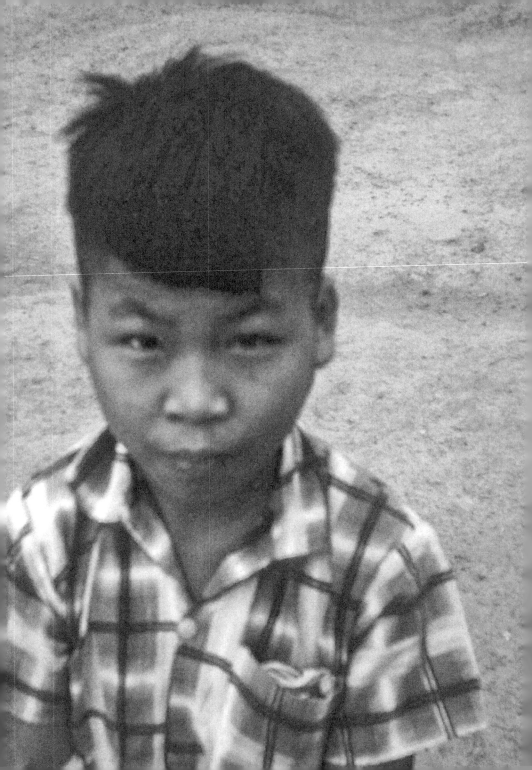

Made in the USA
Middletown, DE
03 September 2024

60118583R00183